HISTORY $^{by}_{the}$ GLASS

Portland's Past and Present Saloons, Bars & Taverns

Paul Pintarich

with a foreword by
Bud Clark

Bianco Publishing

For my father, Paul E. Pintarich, and the stories he has told; my brother, Dick Pintarich, for his historical expertise, research and enthusiasm; Dick Edgington, my best friend and former drinking partner, for transportation and support — and to all those I drank with, sobered up with and who are there to help keep me sober now.

And especially for Clista, my dearest companion, for her love, inspiration and for reminding me that, "From now on, wherever you are is exactly where you should be."

And lastly, for my publisher, Joe Bianco, a long-time colleague and good friend.

Copyright 1996 by Bianco Publishing
P.O. Box 8454
Portland, OR 97207

Cover design by Joe Erceg
Edited by Mary Margaret Hite

ISBN 0-9643408-2-8

Printed in the United States of America

10 9 8 7 6 5 4 3 2

Table of Contents

I.   Foreword .... Bud Clark

II.   Introduction 9

III.   Saloons, Taverns, Pubs & Bars
    The Alibi.. 21
    Capt. Billy Bang's Pub 25
    Buffalo Gap Saloon & Eatery 29
    Caro Amico Italian Café 31
    The Cheerful Tortoise 35
    Cider Mill Restaurant & Lounge 37
    Claudia's 39
    Dad's Restaurant & Lounge 41
    Darcelle XV 45
    Elephant & Castle 49
    Goose Hollow Inn... 51
    Helvetia Tavern 55
    The Horse Brass Pub 57
    Huber's 63
    The Hutch 67
    Jake's Famous Crawfish Restaurant 71
    Jubitz Truck Stop 75
    Kelly's Olympian 79
    Lotus Cardroom & Café 83
    Nick's Famous Coney Island 87
    Nob Hill Bar & Grill 89
    Pal's Shanty 93
    The Portsmouth Club & Lounge 97
    Produce Row Café 99
    Renner's Grill & Lounge 101
    Skyline Tavern 103
    Stanich's Ten-Till-One Tavern; Stanich's West.............. 105

Twilight Room 109

The Vat & Tonsure 111

The Veritable Quandary 115

Wanker's Corner... 117

The White Eagle Café & Saloon 121

IV. The Brothers McMenamin 125

Taverns in My Life

by Bud Clark

As I reminisce now with the hindsight of many good years, it is obvious that taverns have played a most important role in my life.

From my earliest memories of my great-grandfather Johnson, with his daily visits to the corner for his two afternoon beers; from going into the tavern business to support my family and eventually my election as mayor of Portland, as well as the customers and good friends I continue to serve in my own Goose Hollow Inn, taverns have had a profound influence.

When I returned home to Portland after discharge from the Marine Corps in 1954, taverns became my home and playground, where everyone knew my name and I knew theirs.

In those days beer was the drink of choice and the tavern was where you met after school or work. You drank the one beer on tap and talked, argued, and discussed philosophy and the issues of the day with the friendly and not so friendly—all the time hoping to impress the opposite sex—since, after all, that was the most important issue of every day.

Now, Paul Pintarich explores the interesting taverns and saloons that linger in Portland's history; places that represent a living profile of Portland's relatively little-known drinking past, reflecting as well its present and changing future.

The tavern business has changed considerably over the years that I have observed it in Oregon. Improvements in Oregon's liquor laws have stimulated an evolution of taverns, but the entrepreneurial spirit and imagination of barkeepers has also made a difference.

Dorothy McCullough Lee, Portland's first woman mayor, in a reform movement that began in 1949, removed the punch boards, pinball machines and other forms of gambling from Portland taverns, thereby eliminating a steady and lucrative source of income. One oldtime tavern owner told me that in the days of gambling he often "made his nut" before noon, and whatever was earned the rest of the day was pure profit. Eventually the crackdown forced him out of business, since sales of beer alone (nickel and fifteen-cent beers were the norm into the late 1950s) and the heavy competition made it difficult to survive.

Today, however, with the Oregon Lottery encouraging video poker, Keno and other games, many taverns and saloons have been resurrected as little 'casinos.'

During the repressive 1950s, when Oregon liquor laws reflected the lingering morality of Prohibition, taverns could only serve beer on premises, wine only was sold "to go," and the drinking of hard liquor was legal only in "bottle clubs," where patrons were served drinks from bottles they had purchased themselves. Taverns closed at 1 a.m., only recorded music was allowed and customers were restricted by law from singing and dancing, while "nourishment" was, most often, a salty, thirst-inducing offering of chips and nuts.

Not a fun time unless you were a serious drinker not inclined to food and frivolity.

During the next decade, however, tavern owners began experimenting with new strategies to reestablish solvency after the demise of gambling. The price of beer jumped from fifteen to twenty-five cents a glass (though usually a much larger mug) and, to encourage customers, a younger breed of imaginative barkeeps began experimenting with music, food, more exotic beers and wine served with a much-welcomed sense of humor.

Eventually the old laws began to crack, then changed dramatically as customers, more frequently women, were allowed to sing, dance and drink wine and hard liquor by the glass until the wee small hours of the morning.

Entertainment, meanwhile, also enjoyed a "noisy" revolution. On the flip side of a predictable melange of jukebox music, some daring tavern owners began providing only jazz or classical music, while the now legendary and infamous Fungus Room, a brand-new concept in taverns that began in the late '50s, innovated free LP classical music with bartenders acting as DJs. The Fungus Room, a beatnik hangout, had egg cartons on the ceiling to absorb the volume, and "The War of 1812 Overture" cranked to max volume was a crowd favorite.

Pushing the no-entertainment restriction to the edge, Brian Bresslar and Co. offered bartender-comics who performed for the customers beneath flickering silent movies at the now deposed New Old Lompoc House tavern in Old South Portland.

Customers weary of antiquated regulations also helped change the laws, notably Stephen Kafoury, an ebullient state legislator of the time, who in the 1960s became frustrated when he couldn't sing or dance in my own Goose Hollow Inn. Kafoury returned to Salem and changed the law, perhaps becoming Oregon's first legal tavern song-and-dance man.

And food changed too. When I first went into taverns, the closest thing to real food was those tired cellophane-wrapped sandwiches you heated in an infra-red oven. Jerry's Gables, where I once worked as a bartender, made a breakthrough with live hamburgers and eventually began serving full-course dinners. Jerry's was also the first to serve what was then an exotic innovation, "dark beer."

Yours truly, I believe, may have been the first to offer tavern-prepared pizza, now manna to confirmed habitués, in my Spatenhaus Tavern, which was located across from Civic Auditorium where the Ira Keller Fountain is now. I also believe I was the first tavern owner to make hot sandwiches in my pizza oven.

These and other innovations helped to attract a new generation of younger, more playful (and hungrier) customers, who subsequently inspired a new generation of unique Portland taverns.

Taverns have been the social and cultural centers for people throughout the world since civilization began, and will undoubtedly continue as traditional gathering places long into the future. In Portland, my life has been significantly influenced by taverns, both as a patron and owner; my own tavern, through the years, has provided economic stability for myself, a barkeep who became mayor, as well as enabling me to support my family while serving my many friends in a city that I love.

Paul's book takes us through that spectrum of time, a brief historical profile of Portland's older taverns and saloons—drinking places that continue to enhance the unique character of a city I claim proudly as my hometown.

History by the Glass

History by the Glass

When I begin to recall the history of Portland's old saloons, bars and taverns, I think about my father, 82 years old and living in the house he was born in.

He was quite a drinker in his time, the old man. And though both of us downed our last beer years ago, the stories he tells are the yeasty stuff of someone who drank long, hard and frequently in places that are no more.

Many of his stories begin in Michael's Saloon, which before it was overwhelmed by a freeway in the late 1950s was a popular gathering place for the wild young blades of South Portland—notably the old man, whose house is just two blocks away. Built early in the century, Michael's was located on Southwest Corbett Street, near Slavin's Road, and its beer parlor was built on stilts above the tracks of the old Oregon Electric Railway—the "black train," my father called it—overlooking the Willamette River and with a spectacular view east to Mt. Hood.

Throughout its long history, Michael's and its generations of customers represented significant periods of Portland's drinking past. From being a saloon in the bad old days, during Prohibition it became a benign purveyor of soda pop and "near-beer" ("a lot better than some of the real crap they make now days," the old man claims), and after the repeal of Prohibition in 1933, Michael's became a saloon, or tavern, once again.

In its heyday, which according to the old man was when he and his buddies used to drink there (and settled their disputes outside on the corner), it was one of the most popular taverns in town, drawing beers for a clientele attracted from all over the city.

When my father was a boy he and my aunt walked to Michael's for pitchers of birch beer on tap, which my grandfather, who made his own wine, favored while sewing pants and vests in his tailor shop in the family home.

When I was a boy, and Michael's had evolved into a mom-and-pop grocery, I walked with nickels clutched in my hot little hand for the huge ice cream cones they sold there.

Soon after, Michael's simply disappeared.

Today, many years later, looking down from my apartment where I can see my father's house and the overpass where Michael's used to be, I remember those stories and keep them in my mind.

And, remembering, I realize how much the old drinking places of Portland, captured in stories from my father and his father before him, as well as many others—perhaps even my own—have contributed to our city's rich and enduring history.

A "history by the glass."

Who knows for certain when it began?

We may be sure, however, that in the 19th century cutting a city from a stand of virgin timber was thirsty work.

Perhaps some buckskin-clad entrepreneur paddled up the Willamette with a canoe full of booze and began selling it over the top of a stump somewhere? For early Portland was known as "Stumptown," after all.

It was also known as "The Clearing," which by April, 1851, when the city was incorporated, was a clear-cut strip 500 yards wide and one-half mile long: a "rather gamey, one-sided community" of some 800 souls, as it was described; one-sided because 730 of those souls were men, and many of them undoubtedly thirsty.

Within the clearing were 120 one-story frame buildings, including 30 retail and business establishments, six boarding houses, five hotels and eight saloons, including one with billiard tables.

Many early hotels also served liquor, and one of the first was "Pettygrove's," established in 1846 in a double-wide log cabin at the corner of Southwest Taylor Street and Front Avenue. And by 1851, the Warren House Hotel, also on Front Avenue, was advertising in *The Oregonian* (est. 1850) that it offered "the finest liquors and wines."

Portland's first real saloon, however (though again, no one is absolutely certain), was probably that of Colbrun Barnell, a former farmer, who in 1851 was serving drinks from his grocery store on Front Street.

Barnell, who also started Portland's historic Lone Fir Cemetery, was most likely selling liquor supplied by William Ladd, another Portland founder, who arrived the same year with a shipload of booze brought up from San Francisco.

About this time (perhaps because of Ladd's arrival) sprouted Eli Morrill's "Shoe Fly Saloon and Billiard Room," Sam Sykes' colorfully named "Eagle Brewery Depot and Dolly Varden Saloon," Charlie Knowles' "Oro Fino Saloon," as well as the renowned "Eureka Saloon," on Washington Street between First and Second, which *The Oregonian* described confidently (perhaps because of its advertising) as Portland's "original thirst emporium."

Soon there were many more, serving beer provided by the Liberty Brewery (1852), the first in the Northwest; joined in 1856 by Henry Weinhard's City Brewery, now the nationally famous Blitz Weinhard Brewery, which began operations at its present location on Southwest Burnside Street in 1863.

Following custom, Weinhard also owned several saloons: the "Hof Brau," "Oregon Grille," "Quelle Bar," the "Headquarters Saloon" and the "Germania."

(A reminder of those days is Kelly's Olympian, a venerable workingman's bar that remains on Southwest Washington Street, its name lingering from its former direct affiliation with the Olympia Brewery in Tumwater, Wash.)

By the 1870s, when Portland had become a rip-roaring seaport on the West Coast, the city directory listed myriad drinking places, including some, like the notorious "Gulley and Condon Saloon" at Third and B Street, that were harbingers of nastier (some might say more colorful) things to come.

Yet, by that time the city had become less "gamey and one-sided" than before, and from behind a veneer of respectability there were those who felt Portland had too many saloons and sought to shut them down.

The challenge came from the powerful Women's Temperance League of Portland, and in 1874 exploded into "The War of the Webfoot Saloon," an event chronicled in Francis Fuller Victor's book, "The Women's War on Whiskey."

After "three days of chaos," as Fuller described it, the conflict reached a soggy stalemate after Walter Moffett, owner of the Webfoot, located at Southwest First Avenue and Morrison Street, used fire hoses to cool the hotly religious "Leaguers." According to eyewitness accounts, Moffett had incensed the crowd by shouting, "Get out! We don't want any damn whores in here!"

(Another Portland legend claims that the city's ubiquitous drinking fountains, which still bubble on corners downtown, were installed by an old timber baron, Simon Benson, to slake the thirst of his loggers when they came roaring into town.)

But Portland's temperance victory would have to wait until 1914, when Oregon, six years ahead of the nation, would become one of the first states to ratify the Eighteenth (Prohibition) Amendment.

By then, however, Portland had established its reputation as having one of the most notorious waterfronts on the Coast, perhaps even in the world, largely because of the "crimps" who practiced a lucrative trade in providing crews for the sailing ships that called here.

"Shanghaiing" was the term, and no one was more proficient than the infamous "Bunco" Kelly, who operated one of the nefarious sailors' boarding houses that proliferated along the waterfront.

Many an unfortunate sailor—and farmer, logger or otherwise innocent lad just in from the country—awoke after a night of revelry to find himself at sea, having been slipped a "Mickey Finn" and sold to a captain desperate to fill out his crew.

Steamships were coming of age, and sailors who signed on windjammers, which arrived here until the 1920s, were a poorly paid, poorly fed, brutally treated lot who were hard to keep aboard.

Such was Kelly's reputation that a legend persists that he once sold a wooden cigar store Indian to a captain, explaining as he handed over the figure, which was wrapped in a blanket, "Let him sleep for a while. This fellow's really stiff."

Witnesses claim that after the Indian had "slept it off" and was tossed overboard by the irate captain, he was last seen bobbing in the sea, one arm raised stiffly as if waving a grateful goodbye.

Of all of Portland's turn-of-the-century saloons, brothels and boarding houses, however, none remains more legendary than Erickson's, revered in its time as "a cathedral of the working class."

The saloon was established in the 1890s by Augustus "Gus" Erickson, a Russian-Finn and onetime logger, and according to one newspaper account, "It was an institution where men from the great outdoors and the finest gentlemen who ever walked the face of the earth came to meet, drink, gamble, socialize or sample one of the joint's hostesses for a night."

But "joint," certainly, it wasn't.

In its day it was the finest saloon Portland had ever known, a "house of all nations" known around the world, and it was said that if given a choice between Erickson's and Heaven, its patrons would choose Erickson's any day. Erickson's bar was 684 feet long, the longest in the world, and above it was a huge oil painting, "The Slave Market," whose partially clad figures were the toasts of thousands of lonely, hardworked, hard-drinking men.

The saloon covered a full block on Southwest Burnside Street, between Second and Third avenues, and was a city within a city, boasting not only of its bar, billiard room, card room and ice cream parlor, but of its shoeshine stand, restaurant, barber shop, dance hall, and a stage for musicals (with its own orchestra)—and Gus had spent $5,000, a fantastic sum in those days, on a Wurlitzer organ that boomed out over the raucous crowd.

Erickson's even provided its own scrip, which was good for anything purchased inside the saloon, including the ladies who worked upstairs.

For the Dutch lunch that came free with the drinks, Erickson's featured thick slabs of roast ox in sandwiches made from bread baked in its own bakery, which was renowned for its apple pie.

So vital was Erickson's to Portland's saloon society that, during the flood of 1894, when the Willamette River rose to an all-time high and inundated the district, now Portland's Old Town, Erickson's fitted out a raft to serve those undaunted customers who arrived by boat.

But Erickson's had its darker side as well.

Filling six floors in the building above the bar was a combination hotel and brothel, while on the mezzanine were thirteen tiny "cribs" curtained off and available for "quickies." Hard-loving men and women reluctant to leave off from their one-night stands were served food and liquor raised to their rooms by dumbwaiters from the saloon below.

From Erickson's there were also some incidents of Shanghaiing, most likely from the saloon's own drunk tank, which was filled by two formidable bouncers of near-mythical reputation: "Jumbo" Reilly, a man of some 300 pounds who simply sat on miscreants, and the indomitable "Patsy" Cardiff, a former bareknuckled prizefighter who once fought the great John L. Sullivan.

Both, ironically, had reputations for being "soft-spoken" men.

The saloon's grand epoch ended in 1913, however, when the building, since sold by Gus Erickson, was razed following a fire. It was quickly rebuilt by its new owners, Fred Fritz and Jim Russell, but never regained its former splendor.

Though legends of its golden age have endured, Erickson's eventually deteriorated into a skid road bar. Down on his luck, Gus Erickson later worked for Fritz and Russell, but eventually succumed to booze and like his once-great saloon descended onto skid road where he died a common drunk.

Prohibition also ended the golden age of Portland's other saloons. Some became restaurants, like Huber's, the city's oldest, which survives to this day; while others, like Michael's and the more famous Dahl & Penne's, long since gone, simply regrouped to sell soda pop and non-alcoholic beer.

As were other Americans, hardcore Portland drinkers were forced by Prohibition into a demi-monde of speakeasies and bootleggers, home brew and bathtub gin—some finding sustenance in the city's once extensive Chinatown, where they frequented gambling and opium dens. As my father, who admits to having visited such places, pointed out, "Hell, they were all illegal for years anyway."

Immediately following repeal, however, Portland drinkers surfaced to enjoy a proliferation of taverns, bars and nightclubs that overnight seemed to spring up everywhere.

Along Southwest Broadway, for example, much livelier than now (Where can you buy a six-pack in a bank or at Nordstrom's?), my father recalls small joints and larger beer halls packed with customers thirsty for legal beer.

"I bought my first legal beer in Dahl & Penne's," the old man remembers. "They had a bartender left over from saloon days, with a white apron and a long handlebar mustache. That guy was so good he could slide schooners of beer down around the corner of the bar and not spill a drop."

There were singing waiters too, in some places, and the places had names like "The Pub," "The Ratskeller," "Roxy's" and the "Valhalla"— which was on Third Avenue and Burnside Street, across from what used to be Erickson's, and until the late 1950s had replaced Erickson's as the most popular workingman's bar in town.

The "Alaska Card Room and Lunch" was a block away, and also in the old district other bars, clubs and card rooms catering to loggers, working men and pensioners who burrowed into the hotels and rooming houses that identified "skid road."

Skid road, as Northwest historians will remind you most adamantly, is a regional term never to be confused with "skid row," a more generic label used today to identify down-and-out districts almost anywhere.

Portland's was the original skid road (though Seattle's Pike Street claims to be a contender), harkening back to much earlier days, when loggers used teams of oxen to skid logs down along a greased track from the West Hills to the waterfront (though by the 1940s and '50s much of Portland's skid road had evolved, or deteriorated—depending on who you talk to)—into a more desperately verifiable skid row).

The Valhalla remained, along with a whiff of old Erickson's, but skid row was identified now by such dangerous and hard-drinking places as "The Caribou Club" (recently revived in name only), the "Apache Club" ("Check all knives and guns at the bar," read a sign over the bar), "The Lotus" (recently gentrified), "The Old Glory" (no longer waving—thank God!), "The Stockman's Club," "Little Brown Jug," "Dinty Moore's," and a plethora of other dowdy bars, taverns, card rooms and former saloons.

Many have disappeared, though others, with names retained from the past, are being transformed into hip, trendy places as skid row becomes Old Town, its fortified winos slowly replaced by clearer-eyed, more affluent individuals who "do lunch" and prefer wines of a gentler vintage.

World War II revitalized Portland. Its humming shipyards attracted thousands of workers from across the country, the vanguard of our present population boom, and these were later joined by servicemen and merchant seamen, who had visited during the war and now returned to live in the bustling port city.

Portland was a friendly and lively place during the war, and after the long Depression, with everyone working round-the-clock in the war economy, people had money, and they spent a lot of it on booze.

My father remembers the activity, the streets crowded with people night and day, filling the nightclubs and dance halls, which attracted the big-name big bands of the day: the Dorsey Brothers, Harry James, Woody Herman, Benny Goodman and Artie Shaw, playing for crowds at the Jantzen Beach Ballroom, McElroy's, the Uptown and Crystal ballrooms—and many more.

Portland nightclubs were jumpy and jivey, and seemed to be on every corner downtown: places like the bamboo-infested "Zombie Zulu," the "Pago Pago," "Club Portland" and the "Clover Club," "Amatos," the

"Diamond Horseshoe," the Washington Hotel's "Timber Topper," and the "Rose Garden," in Portland's once-fashionable Multnomah Hotel.

And many more, too many and too long ago to recall.

Until the early 1950s, most Portland nightspots were "bottle clubs." This required that you bring your own bottle (purchased with a license at a state-owned liquor store, or "green front") and check it with the bartender who sold you "setups" of mixer and ice.

Meanwhile, lurking on the dark side of respectability were a number of after-hours joints, shadowy places like Tom "Pop" Johnson's "Blackberry Patch," "Barney Kay's" and "Rampoos," where you brought your own bottle and could drink until dawn.

Until the '50s encouraged the automobile-driven diaspora of suburban sprawl, finding action in Portland meant, for the most part (there were roadhouses), going downtown. For no matter how much you had drunk, the wonderful old streetcars would get you home.

Most Portlanders then lived conveniently close to the urban core, however, and denizens of the city's still quite liveable neighborhoods enjoyed the conviviality of corner taverns, many of which, in original or altered versions, remain today: unique interpretations of what an American pub might be.

But back in their bad old days, before the reforms of the infamous Dorothy McCullough Lee, the taverns were unique in many other ways as well. According to former Mayor Bud Clark, who has owned Portland's popular Goose Hollow Inn for many years, some were little more than gambling dens offering games of chance in the form of punchboards, and payoffs to high rollers who scored on the once ubiquitous pinball machines.

The militant Mayor Lee would change all that—though now she might roll over in her grave. Ironically, now, with Oregon's State Lottery games, taverns, bars and clubs are often chancier than they were before.

The straight-laced '50s are also remembered for the decade's oppressive ambiance. Though it may seem ridiculous to the young exuberant drinkers of today, singing was not allowed, nor was dancing and live music. In those days you hummed quietly, whistled under your breath or tapped your toes (softly) to tunes restricted to the jukebox.

(Ironically, with all these restrictions, children were allowed in taverns with their parents, and I remember spending some of my formative years bellied up to the bar next to the old man.)

Then, in the late '50s, at the beginning of my own drinking days, thing began to change. After four years in the service, returning with a thirst that seems dangerous to me now (and was), I would soon see my hometown's drinking places dramatically transformed.

Oh sure, some of the old nightclubs remained, but they were fading, giving way to some newer, more vibrant, often rowdier clubs—"Elmo's," "The Turquoise Room," the "Three Star" and "The Town Mart" come to mind—while other chic watering holes were springing up with the growth of suburbia.

But downtown in Old Town, near Union Station, no place was filled with more fun than Harvey Dick's lively, vastly entertaining and richly fitted out Hoyt Hotel, still a wonderful memory though it has been gone for more than thirty years. Not since the heyday of Erickson's had Portland seen such splendor: a grand and glorious, brashly irreverent, no-holds barred watering hole that rocked with elaborate floor shows and rolled with the infectious laughter of its irrepressible impresario, the legendary Gracie Hansen.

If suddenly resurrected in the Hoyt, the spirits of men who had sought Heaven in Erickson's would find paradise in the hotel's gas-lighted Barbary Coast and Roaring Twenties rooms; in a restaurant with thick steaks you could select yourself; or in the Hoyt's exclusive Men's Bar—where today's feminists might die, perhaps thinking themselves in hell.

Dick was an entrepreneur of ribald humor, and his Men's Bar restroom was fitted out with an inspiring running waterfall, and next to it a gaping-mouth bust of Cuban dictator Fidel Castro for inspiration of a different kind.

I once spent a New Year's Eve there and I'm recovering from it still. Once, I interviewed actress Jane Russell there, and Miss Russell, who had been around, told me she'd never seen anything like it.

Nor, I replied, had I.

Particularly one night in the Men's Bar, when, drinking with my father after a rather bizarre evening, we prevented our guest, a frolicksome Croatian ship's officer and Russian-trained ballet dancer, from plunging a wickedly long knife into the capacious girth of a man blowing cigar smoke in his face.

Grabbing him from each side, we hustled him out to the sidewalk, where he displayed a masterful pirouette and sang a few loud bars from "I Pagliacci" in Serbo-Croatian before we put him in a cab and sent him back to his ship.

True story; but everyone who has been there has stories of their own, for it was that kind of place: delicious, decadent, sometimes dangerous, but…oh, such fun!

The art of stripping, or "exotic dancing," as we know it today, was taking off about this time and oldtimers remember the talents of such memorable ecdysiasts (H.L. Mencken's term) as The White Fury, Jeannie the Bikini (she of the whirling tassels), the Eiffel Tower Girl and the immortal Tempest Storm, whose blazing red hair lighted the runway at the old Star Theater. Their legacy would be assumed by a short-lived phenomenon known as "go-go dancing," with the genre grinding eventually into today's bumper crop of totally nude (and totally artless) "dancers" who adhere to the dictum that "less is more."

More or less.

And for less there is still "Mary's Club," a resilient strip club on lower Southwest Broadway, where as a young police reporter I once spent Christmas morning among a group of desperate, heavy-breathing men, all of whom I remember wearing sunglasses.

From personal observations, however, I came to realize that more is often better in matters erotic, especially as I grew older. Still locked in my fantasies is a beautiful young blonde woman who danced above the bar at "Ray's Helm" years ago, when it was a popular jazz club on Northeast Broadway. Wearing nothing but a skirt, sweater, high heels and a single strand of pearls, she danced with the sensual abandon of a secretary at a Christmas party, lifting the roof off the place and driving me wild.

About this time Portland had acquired a well-deserved national reputation as a jazz town. There was an abundance of local talent, and the city attracted nationally known musicians who were featured in clubs like Ray's (with vocalist-pianist Jeannie Hoffman and her partner, bass player Bill Knuckles) and others, including "The Hobbit," "Parchman Farm," "The Jazz Quarry" (with the venerable Eddie Weed), and "Sidney's," owned by Sidney Porter, an extremely tall, thin, long-fingered pianist of consummate skill, who featured vocals by his wife Nola, who sang like a bird.

(I remember bouncing into Sidney's late at night to be greeted by Sidney, who would require that I wear one of his sports coats for the evening. I am six-feet-four, but Sidney's coats dangled to my knees and the sleeves covered my hands.)

Good music and dancing could also be found in Portland's black district, which in the old days was concentrated along North Williams Avenue and had grown considerably following the influx of shipyard workers up from the South during World War II.

Black clubs jumped to a rhythm of their own, and in those days invited white customers to lively places like the "Cotton Club," the "Savoy," "McLendon's Rhythm Room" and "Geneva's," where both races mingled congenially, but places, sadly, that are no more.

"Those days were somethin'," says my old friend Mary Lockridge, who at 80 still sings around town and bills herself as "The Million-Dollar Grandma."

"I knew all them people then," she said. "I knew Pop Johnson, I grew up with Sidney Porter's family...all of those oldtime black Portland families, I knew 'em. It was different then. I used to sing at the old Desert Room. Everybody had a great time, black and white. It wasn't like nowadays. You remember?"

I do, but that's a story I'm not going to tell here.

Gone, too, are the Beatniks.

Remember them?

They were big back in the '50s, favoring dark clothes, black berets and grim expressions to remind themselves that life at best was an absurd existential nightmare—at least until you drank enough beer.

"Grass" was good, cheap, but hard to get, and until the 1960s, wine and beer were their drugs of choice. The beer was dark, like the stuff drunk by Kerouac and company down in "Vesuvio's" ("we're glad to get out of Portland, Oregon," the sign read) or the "Co-Existence Bagel Shop," both down in San Francisco where the whole beatnik thing began.

Portland's beatniks, never a large contingent, gathered like moths around the dim flame of the appropriately named "Fungus Room" in Old South Portland, where they snapped their fingers (remember that?) in appreciation of the classical music played by the room's bartender.

Compared to the pap available on most tavern juke boxes, classical music was an innovation right up there with dark beer, and when the oft-requested "War of 1812 Overture" was cranked up, fingers must have snapped like a swarm of crickets in heat.

Though its existential angst was brief, the Fungus Room inspired dramatic changes in Portland's tavern scene as it moved into an era of beards, bell bottoms and beads, while folk singers sang laments of social and ethnic concern.

By the time the '50s became the '60s, and the beatniks had metamorphosed into "hippies" (hippies, according to Ken Kesey, Oregon author and former Merry Prankster, being beatniks who didn't know how to read) the city's taverns were rife with innovations encouraged by more daring barkeeps. At "The New Old Lompoc House," for example, which was near the Fungus Room, comedian Brian Bresslar (who would later appear on "Laugh In") offered customers silent movies with their popcorn and dark beer, which he served along with jerky imitations of the actors on the screen.

Just up the street, hamburgers were being served to beer drinkers at "Jerry's Gables," as they were at "Montgomery Gardens," over by Portland State College (it wasn't a university yet), where on Fridays poor students like myself could forget a week of classes over glasses of nickel beer.

PSC students and the old neighborhood denizens they drank with were blessed with a bounty of taverns that would soon be swept away by the I-405 freeway and the school's own rapid metastasis eating into what was once a sweetly comfortable downtown community.

Within lurching distance of each other were "The Cheerful Tortoise" (expanded, but still on its corner), the "Round Robin," "Green Spot," "The

Chocolate Moose" (whose owner's proboscis matched exactly the shape of his tavern's stuffed namesake on the wall), and "Lydia's," with its matchless Reuben sandwiches, and later, "Sam's Hofbrau"—all of them college hang-outs raucous with laughter and conversation that drifted through clouds of smoke floating above an ocean of beer.

Just down the street, across from *The Oregonian*, was the "Broadway Inn," a hangout for newspapermen, where Jeannie twirled her tassels above cynical ink-stained wretches discussing the agonies of their days, and in the other direction, across from Civic Stadium and adjacent to the City Morgue, Bud Clark's first tavern, "The Spatenhaus."

Though Portland was introduced to pizza at the "Caro Amico" restaurant in 1949, Clark claims his Spatenhaus was the first tavern in the city to serve pizza, now a ubiquitous staple of tavern life.

Old Portlanders will also recall "Shakey's Original Pizza Parlor," on Southeast Foster Road, which before its recent demise spawned a chain of knock-offs that stretched from coast to coast.

Also about this time, Oregon tavern rats were cheering the State Legislature for easing restrictions to allow singing and dancing, live music, later hours and the serving of wine, all of which enticed more women into a new age of wine and song (the ferns would come later), to the delight of everyone.

And while many neighborhood taverns stubbornly retained their funky character, dear to the hearts of oldtime customers, many of whom inherited the stools of their fathers and grandfathers, newer places appeared with characteristics more appealing to the young at heart.

"The Wurst Haus," my favorite watering hole for a time, had pizza, chessboards and classical music on the juke; the little-known "Netcap Tavern" was on stilts overlooking the river (it burned when its owner tried thawing pipes with a blow torch); "Dante's Inferno" in South Portland featured "Chef Gino" (formerly of the Wurst Haus) and a menu of international delights; you could drop in and chat up the ladies at the "Blind Onion," out on Northeast Broadway, or in "The Dandelion Pub," in Portland's Uptown district; while at Bud Clark's "Goose Hollow Inn..."

Well, everybody knows about "The Goose," still attracting gaggles of drinkers after all these years.

Sports fans could catch the Tuesday night turtle races at "The Faucet" out in Raleigh Hills, mingle with a loud profusion of jocks in "Claudia's," Portland's original sports bar, and once the most popular tavern in town, out on Southeast Hawthorne Boulevard; and farther up the boulevard, drop in for a "coney" and talk baseball with Frank Nudo at "Nick's Coney Island," a remnant of the late '40s that remains unchanged after all these years.

Moving downtown, one could find "Peter's Inn" and "Peter's Out," sports bars owned by former professional baseball player Frank Peters, a glib, lively but now infamous raconteur who for a time was Portland's version of "Cheers" bartender Sam Malone.

And on the city's underbelly were places I remember from my days as a young police reporter: "Kelly's," "The Harvester," "O'Connor's" (the old one), the "Golden Dragon," "George's," "Van's," "Tom's," "Bob's," "Nobby's," "The Lovejoy," "The New Moon," "Hal's" "Satan's Cellar," "LeFebvre's;" while on the way home I might stop at "The High Time," "The Chat-n-Nibble," "The Cider Mill," "The Firestone," "The Ship," the "Leipzig" and "Pogo's" in Moreland...and others, ad infinitum, which I've simply forgotten.

But I'll never forget "Renner's," in Multnomah Village, where I drank my last beer—my last drink ever—nearly 14 years ago.

God! I must have been thirsty.

Today, as they have in the past, Portland's drinking places are changing significantly, as are their customers, who, unlike myself and my former hard-drinking companions, are for the most part saner, wiser and less apt to drink themselves to oblivion, or death—and try to drive there afterwards.

In the following selection of Portland's older saloons, bars and taverns, the barkeepers themselves, a surprising number of them natives to the city, describe the changes they have seen over the years.

Generally you will find that customers are getting what they desire: unique atmosphere, friendly service and finer food, and most important of all, a wide and interesting variety of high-quality wines, liquor and beers, both foreign and domestic.

Right now, as you shall see, Portland (some call it "Beer City") has a greater number of microbreweries and brewpubs per capita than any other city in the United States, and Oregon ranks second only to Belgium in having more microbreweries per capita than any country in the world.

Recognizing the number of fine new microbreweries and brew pubs going on tap each year, we may also assume that Portlanders have become the most discriminating beer drinkers in the world; drinking less, certainly, but perhaps doing more to enhance and refine the city's long and colorful drinking history.

A "history by the glass."

The Alibi

4024 N. Interstate Ave.
503-287-5335

What a surprise to discover that I once met Roy Ell, legendary former owner of The Alibi, way back in the 1950s when Ell was transforming the popular North Portland night spot into the highly successful restaurant and lounge it remains today.

I was a young sailor then, hitchhiking up from the Coast, and I remember Ell as a smallish man who invited me into his big car and gave me a lift to town.

It was a rainy, windy day, and against the slap of the windshield wipers, Ell's car winding through the Coast Range, he asked why I was going to Portland and what business I might have there.

When I told him Portland was my home and that I returned often for weekend liberty, Ell's eyes brightened and he cut me a warm smile.

"Then you must stop by my place," he said. "I own The Alibi, out on Interstate. You come in and the drinks are on me."

Forty years later I show up at The Alibi and wonder why it took me so long. I guess because I'm a Westside person, and in Portland oldtimers' allegiances, even to taverns, are more often determined by which side of the river they come from.

Ell is gone now anyway, and it's okay because I gave up drinking a long time ago.

That's my Alibi.

But Ell is not forgotten. Mention the former owner to Larry White, who took over in 1992, and Ell's name becomes the stuff of legend; a success story that began in 1947 when Ell leased a small roadside tavern and within a few short years created what White refers to as a "tropical paradise."

That's right. Among the starker realities of this otherwise prosaic, workaday North Portland neighborhood, The Alibi is an exotic Polynesian incongruity drifted ashore along Interstate Avenue.

"Hang ten" on the damp sidewalk of a gray Northwest day, ride an existential curl through the Alibi's carved wooden door, and it's "Aloha" all over the place: instant Waikiki with "A Little Grass Shack" ambiance that transports the visitor to the South Seas.

(Or at least, a loosely interpreted facsimile thereof.)

Looking around, it is hard to believe that this was once a rest stop for horse-and-buggy traffic along what was known as the "Interstate Trail" back in the late 19th century; a route that, before the I-5 freeway, later became Highway 99 and the main road north to Seattle.

That first rest stop was called the "Chat-n-Nibble," and by the time Ell took over it was "The Max Alibi," a tiny tavern named after its second owner, Max Peterson.

How it looks today reflects Ell's love of the islands, White explains, and The Alibi remains a reliquary for his passion: totems and tiki torches, monster clam shells that used to grab natives in old movies, nets of course, and lots of grass and bamboo, along with carved masks, spears and other relics accompanied by the small splashing of falling water.

So naturally it's no surprise when White comes forth wearing a blue Hawaiian shirt, one of those authentic creations with coconut shell buttons that seems to have been conceived in a beachcomber's dream.

A youthful 42, White is a tanned, in-shape-looking man who, with his clipped gray hair, mustache and that wallpaper shirt, might be mistaken for a hip kind of Hollywood guy rather than a native Oregonian born close to Tillamook Bay.

Breaking a small smile, White leans across his cluttered desk in an office hidden behind the Alibi's kitchen, speaking softly, like a man about to cut you in on a deal.

White tells you he began in the restaurant business at seventeen, enlisting as a private in one of the Colonel's fried chicken outfits down at the Coast. Hooked by the smell of grease and the roar of hungry customers chowing down, White rose through the ranks to eventually move out and become a manager of restaurants, first in Southern Oregon, then up here closer to town.

"Then I saw an ad for a manager's job at The Alibi and decided to inquire," says White, who had long been aware of The Alibi's enduring popularity; its varied menu and exotic lounge, its authentic tropical atmosphere sustaining success in the house that Ell built.

"I liked that," he says simply, continuing his story of how he became friends with Roy Ell.

History by the Glass

"I came in one day during lunch and the place was 'packed out,' a couple of employees having not shown up that day," he said. "I just jumped in and helped out. I said, 'follow me, do what I do...' And after about two hours Roy walks in and introduces himself. After looking around, he tells the others, 'If it hadn't been for Larry you wouldn't have made it today.'

"Then to me he says, 'Let's talk.'"

Since that day, White admits, Ell's dream has become his own.

"I like it," he says, "It's in my blood."

White gets up and I follow his tropical shirt back into the cozy, water-tinkling gloom that tosses back memories from the years I spent in the Islands; in the Navy back in the '50s, not too long after that rainy day ride with Roy Ell through the Coast Range.

Lunch is underway, a few early drinkers have washed up along the bar and the poker machines have begun feeding like hammerhead sharks.

White is more expansive now, moving his arms and pointing out the booths, the small café off to the side, proffering a menu crowded with old favorites: chicken, beef, pork and, catering to the ambiance, shelled creatures and two-eyed steak from the sea.

Crossing the bar (a tropical fish tank there) assures you of adventures in drinking: fruity, umbrella-shaded esoterica redolent of pineapple and papaya—"We're famous for our mai tais," White explains—but also the straight-up harder stuff, including a respectable representation of local beers.

The Alibi has always been popular in the North Portland neighborhood, and from nearby Swan Island, with its industrial parks and Port of Portland facilities, come after-workers who for decades have made this a favorite watering hole.

And now something new, White explains, after being asked if it isn't awfully quiet around here now—a swelling crowd up and over from downtown.

"It's been word-of-mouth," he says. "People started coming up after the Blazer (Portland Trail Blazer basketball team) games, then because a lot of places aren't open downtown anymore. We're not that far away, and people want to get away to an exotic place. The limo drivers know us and bring them here."

White has a staff of seventeen, a crew described by The Alibi's owner as having "personality, integrity and honesty; people our customers come back for. We're here to serve and entertain—and the food's good."

Open each day from 11 a.m. to 2:30 a.m. (1 a.m. on Sunday), The Alibi hums at noon and during the evenings, but picks up a throb on Wednesdays that lasts through the weekend. The uninhibited may belt songs into The Alibi's karaoke machine, and Thursday and Saturday nights. White brings in a DJ to spin out tunes, mostly music for a younger crowd.

"We know how to throw a party," he says proudly, "and we do a lot of them: birthdays, anniversaries, engagements…We're getting customers now whose parents still come in here."

Walking toward the door, where to go outside means taking a quantum leap from gentle tradewinds to where the North Wind blows, I stop, turn back and half-expect White to call out "aloha."

Instead he grins and says softly, "If they ask, tell them we're a 'Kon-Tiki' type of restaurant. And if they like the Islands, tell them to come here."

Capt. Billy Bang's Pub

5331 S.W. Macadam Ave.
503-227-4663

When I first met Bob Gekler we were both much younger, and Bob owned and operated The Dandelion Pub, a stylish and popular bar and restaurant in Northwest Portland's Uptown Shopping Center.

That was about thirty years ago, in a period in my life when I was a hard-drinking newspaperman and The Dandelion was one of the newer, more fashionable bars popping up all over the city.

To me, The Dandelion provided refuge and relief from the "usual suspects" who were often my drinking companions in the harder-core bars farther downtown. The Dandelion offered good food, music and an atmosphere conducive to reflection and conversation, a rare commodity in most Portland bars and taverns these days.

It was in The Dandelion too that I often encountered former classmates of mine from Lincoln High School (Gekler's alma mater as well); many of whom, I was dismayed to discover, had opted for bland careers in selling insurance, and whose chagrin was apparent after I told them I was intent on drinking all the beer in world while pursuing a goal of becoming a pastoral poet.

"Look here," a renewed acquaintance once inquired as we sat at The Dandelion's congenial bar, "Have you given any thought to 'thirty paid life?' "

"Look here," I countered, "Have you ever read *Zorba the Greek*?"

Though I had occasionally frequented Bob's subsequent enterprises, notably the tony Polish Princess restaurant, as well as a downtown nightspot called Naughty Jane's, both of which are now history, I caught up with Bob years later in his Capt. Billy Bang's Pub, a convivial oasis lurking among the multifarious establishments within the labyrinthine passageways of The Water Tower arcade at John's Landing.

Not surprisingly, I felt right at home in Billy Bang's, for this was all my family's neighborhood around here. My mother and father had grown up on the same street two blocks away, my maternal grandfather had once been chief sawyer at the now long gone Jones Lumber Co., a bit farther down Macadam Avenue, and my other grandfather, a custom tailor, had his shop in the family home up the hill, where my father was born and lives today.

And there was Bob at the bar, bearded and a bit grayer at 71; slowed somewhat by time but friendly, knowledgeable and, occasionally, as irascible as ever.

While not a pub in the classical sense—Gekler describes it as a "Northwest contemporary pub"—Billy Bang's hints at British coziness with its captain's chairs, snug booths and tables wrapped into an atmosphere made cool by dark wood paneling.

Gekler, who retains a city-wide reputation as a venerable, if not classy, entrepreneur, reveals his personal aesthetic in Billy Bang's cobbled outdoor terrace, which he describes as "the prettiest in town."

He also emphasizes that the pub not be described as a "meet market," but as a place that offers a wholesome and vibrant ambiance inviting to customers of all tastes and ages.

Which it is, particularly on evenings and weekends when a lot of younger people are crouching over the pub's two pool tables or gathered in warm conviviality around the U-shaped bar, where less hurried neighborhood codgers like myself are often found mingling comfortably with fast-track, suburban-bound yuppies washed in from the frenetic commuter stream.

Prominent as well is what Gekler refers to as a "loyal contingent" of bar, tavern and restaurant employees, who come here to relax after working shifts in the myriad restaurants, bars and saloons burgeoning throughout the revived Southwest Portland neighborhood.

Somewhat proudly, Gekler says, "We're kind of a club for the people who work around here," before chomping bites out of a monster sandwich from the pub's kitchen.

The pub has an eclectically trendy menu, and features a varied and appealing brunch on weekends, with tables available on the coveted terrace when the Oregon weather is kind.

A lot of beer washes over Billy Bang's bar, but so does a lot of hard liquor mixed into drinks both predictable (for the older, hard core drinkers) and hipper, often phantasmagorical concoctions for those just learning to wet their whistle.

Drunks are seldom in evidence, or are well behaved, and weekend afternoons hum softly with a drone of tired shoppers and neighborhood denizens, the whole orchestrated with background music or the subdued roar of a sports event on the tube.

Weekday afternoons often see denizens like myself, retired or simply tired ladies and gentlemen sharing experiences and philosophies learned after years of enduring life's fair and stormy weather.

Gekler, a native of Portland, knows his city well. He was once a habitué of downtown, where he learned the streets and their secrets as a hustling young messenger back in the '30s and '40s, and later, after serving in the Navy during World War II, as owner of several popular restaurants and bars.

Today, however, only Billy Bang's remains under the tender care of Gekler, who is often found there in the early afternoon, and who, with little encouragement, very willingly relates raspy-voiced stories of how things in Portland used to be.

"Hey! Come over here! You remember Tommy Luke? The florist guy? Well, during Prohibition Tommy got his start . . . But, ah hell, I'd better not tell you that one," he chuckles, his memory mixing scandals and secrets into the rich old stories of time.

Once not so long ago, when the trendy John's Landing building was a monster factory instead, you could look out the window and see a South Portland that was a bustling neighborhood of lumber mills and furniture factories. Its resident work force thrived in small single-family homes and boarding houses, and at the end of the day they relaxed in a number of long-established, sometimes legendary taverns and saloons.

In the 1970s, however, there began a dramatic transformation that brought a brash new wave of condos, apartments and townhouses into the neighborhood, resulting in a cultural collision that drew fire from some of its more entrenched denizens.

"Can you believe it? People didn't want me in here at first," Gekler, a likeable curmudgeon, admits. "There were a lot of complaints, and even some vandalism," he adds with a chuckle that tells you now everything is okay.

"Then I hired two of the toughest kids in the neighborhood to watch out for things. I had no more trouble after that. In fact, one of those kids became the best cook I ever had."

Gekler observes realistically that a lot of neighborhood newcomers (many residing in a virtual glut of high-priced row houses) are infrequent visitors of Billy Bang's.

Nor, he complains mildly, does he capture as many as he would like of the stressed-out rush-hour commuters zipping by on the Macadam Avenue main line (ironically, once a major Indian trail alongside the

Willamette River), bound for the upper-scale watering holes of the farther-out suburban communities.

"Yet," he laments resignedly, "I guess we've created our own traffic problems. There are just too many cars, and the places you used to get to easily you just can't get to anymore. It hurt downtown and it's hurting us here as well."

Yet not that much, for business is still good, Billy Bang's customers seem cheerful, loyal and satisfied, and, despite Gekler's protestations, most have arrived in their cars.

Pick a nice day, or even better a rainy one, and if you suddenly find yourself relaxing around Capt. Billy Bang's comfortable bar or outside on its cobbled terrace—"the prettiest in town"—you will soon understand why the stop is worthwhile.

Buffalo Gap
Saloon & Eatery

6835 S.W. Macadam Ave.
503-244-7111

Joe G. Bianco

Wait a minute! This is all wrong in here. What are these buffalo heads and all this Great Plains stuff (isn't that a photograph of Sitting Bull?) doing in a tavern in the rainy Northwest?

And why "Buffalo Gap," for God's sake, instead of some name evocative of trees, rain, salmon and webbed feet?

"Quack! Quack!" A native Oregonian is tempted to squawk.

Yeah, yeah...okay! Owner Jack Stutzman takes the blame, a native of South Dakota who took over the place in 1973 when it was the "Hoot Owl," but whose mood drifted back to the High Plains a year later after he changed the name and "started in with the cowboys, buffaloes and all of that..."

Many locals like myself remember the place as "Bob's Tavern," a desperately lighted, single-pool table kind of place as cheery as a painting by Edward Hopper.

In those days, back when we were under-age hellions, South Portland was a leaner, meaner, less trendy place and Willamette Park, just across the way, was a cottonwood swamp where we dodged the law and high water to chug down six-packs of ill-gotten beer.

But around here it's not that way anymore. Bob's is gone, along with the "Home Tavern," the "Netcap Tavern," the ill-lighted but good-feeding "Dante's Inferno," as well as other places of nefarious ilk, replaced increasingly by upscale taverns like this one here.

Stutzman, a man in his 50s "and holding," as they say, has been a tavern and bar owner in Portland long enough to be naturalized. With imagination and entrepreneurial daring, he has widened the once narrow Buffalo Gap into a multifarious "saloon and eatery" that invites its patrons young and old (children are allowed in certain areas before 9 p.m.) to wallow in an environment Stutzman proclaims is "as eclectic as possible."

Within a buffalo chip's toss of the Willamette River, where we once guzzled Oly and Blitz, the Gap has three full-sized pool tables, a restaurant, full bar, cozy nooks and crannies, as well as a fully serviced upstairs that used to be a brothel in the old days, and now includes another bar and space for live music featured Wednesday through Saturday nights.

Stutzman describes the music offerings as "jazz-bluesy-folksy-Rocky Mountain…or whatever?…but the listening kind," he emphasizes.

And while there is no dance floor upstairs (or down), buffalo hunters may cut out from the herd enough buffalo gals to make the climb worthwhile.

Found upstairs as well is an outdoor terrace with tables and umbrellas, with a view that has inspired the owner to proclaim imperiously, "You are high atop the Stutzman Building, overlooking the mighty Willamette!"

Though Stutzman also proclaims hiply that "brunch is not us," the Gap offers an extensive menu of what the owner describes as "American diner cuisine," or "tavern food," ideal for those who have a cholesterol count of, say, 20. With weekend brunch gone the way of the buffalo, breakfast is, however, served seven days a week.

Filling the Gap are two full bars and six beers on tap, including a representation of Oregon's microbreweries, though like most other Portland taverns these days more business is done with food.

When he's off the phone, which is rarely, Stutzman is a trove of information about the Portland tavern scene, of which he played no little part.

Back in the late 1950s he owned the popular "Green Spot Tavern," since gobbled up by Portland State University, and was owner of "The Local Gentry" and "Gassy Jack's." He remembers how it used to be then, when people *really* drank, but will tell you it's better now…and certainly much safer.

In a cluttered office walled with old barn wood, stacked with Big Sky bibelots and dominated by the well-endowed sculpted nude torso of a former Green Spot customer (female), Stutzman admits, "there's no such thing as a 'tavern scene' in Portland anymore."

The reference is to when he and many others, including myself, were younger, wilder and crazier, and shared a dangerous camaraderie with people we knew all over town.

"It's all changed," he says somewhat sadly, yet adding quickly, "though this is a happy bar. And I intend to keep it that way. My goal is to be here for another twenty years."

Symbolizing this commitment, Stutzman recently added the "Badlands' Chili Parlor" as an enhancement of the Buffalo Gap's atmosphere, which already reeks heavily of the dry Great Plains.

But in two more decades…who knows?

Beneath all this Oregon rain he may finally come around.

"Quack! Quack…"

Caro Amico Italian Café

3606 S.W. Barbur Blvd.
503-223-6895

"It was a dark and stormy night..."
...and cold, and a long, long time ago when I and several teenage friends took a break from our mild vandalism of loosening fireplugs throughout the South Portland neighborhood and decided upon a pizza.

"Pizza?" we inquired of one of our more worldly companions, as we conferred in the chill heavy spray spouting from a plug released alongside Barbur Boulevard.

"Yeah, pizza!" he snorted with disbelief. "Geez! You know. Those flat, round Italian bread things covered with tomato sauce and cheese...?"

But we didn't know, for we were Portland kids and in the Portland of my youth pizza was still a mostly rumored delicacy just oozing its way West out of the ethnic neighborhoods of the East.

In that time, the early '50s, before Elvis and prior to the primordial strains of rock-and-roll, there was only one restaurant in all of Portland that served pizza pie: the Caro Amico—which, on that cold wet night so long ago, we could see gleaming warmly right across the street.

Between the four of us we collected a handful of pocket change, and after hiding the fireplug wrench (we found it) scurried across Barbur Boulevard and entered the modest front door, there to be overcome by the dark warmth, the cloying smells of herbs and spices redolent with the funky ambiance of our night's work.

And the pizza? It exploded on our unjaded palates like Vesuvius. Thin it was, and crispy crusted, hot cheese and meat all melted into itself; an exotic concoction of tastes and aromas that made us believers for evermore: the Caro Amico—a large pizza then was only $1.50!

Opened in 1949 on the same spot where it stands today, the old Caro Amico was different only in its architecture. In those days, before it burned some years later, it was in a tall Victorian house on the edge of an old Italian-Jewish neighborhood, its dimly lighted presence more like a bordello than the Baker Family restaurant it remains today.

Being teenage romantics, we also liked the shadowy implications that perhaps something was going on there that shouldn't be (which was close to the truth, it later turned out).

The current proprietor, Elsie Baker McFarland, daughter of Caro Amico founder Fred Baker, hints at some long-ago mischief (maybe an illegal liquor or backroom gambling joint?), planned possibly by her father and his original partner, Joe Fracasso, back in the richly textured Victorian house days.

Today, however, lingering myths and rumors only enhance the character of a Portland institution whose venerability is firmly established after nearly fifty years.

Sitting out on the restaurant's back deck, where if you look carefully there is a South Portland view of Mt. Hood and the Ross Island Bridge, Elsie looks up at the recently painted "new" Caro Amico that rose from old ashes some years ago.

"It hasn't changed that much," Elsie, an attractive, athletic woman in her early sixties, says with a gentle smile. "This is Portland's original pizzeria, and it has kept a classic '50s–'60s feeling."

The feeling is retained in the older lower part of the restaurant with its big-windowed views to the river and mountains, and in its cozy bar, a hangout for young people who mingle with old neighborhood survivors as well as with graying, middle-aged citizens like me who ate pizzas here when we were in high school.

After games, proms and that once unique, now-disappeared Portland mating ritual known as "dragging Broadway," teenagers descended on the Caro Amico from schools all over the city, gobbling pizza and leaving their American graffiti on the restaurant's famed red paper lampshades that, alas, are no more.

"People miss the lampshades," Elsie admits ruefully. "There were thousands of names written there, and many would like to see them back. But…" she sighs, "times change."

As its slogan implies, Caro Amico is truly a place "Where Dear Friends Meet." Caro Amico means "Dear Friend" in Italian, of course, and Elsie smiles at the incongruity of one of Portland's oldest Italian restaurants being owned by a family that is not Italian at all.

In fact, Elsie's grandfather, Benjamin Franklin Baker, was a pioneer who homesteaded on Pete's Mountain, near the farming community of Canby on the Willamette River, which is some miles south of here.

Her father, Fred, had been a purser on the old riverboats but left the water and returned to the homestead to raise Elsie and her three brothers, as well as coterie of farm animals, including a large flock of chickens whose eggs he sold on a regular route through Portland.

Among Fred Baker's customers were a number of Italians, including his future partner, Joe Fracasso, whose family already owned the legendary but now-defunct Prima Donna restaurant farther down Fourth Avenue, a little closer to town.

"Joe Fracasso wanted a place where he could serve pizza," Elsie explains. "They didn't have pizza at the Prima Donna because Joe's mother, Mary, didn't want to do pizza there for some reason," she adds with a smile and an Italianate tossing of her hands.

For the first two or three years the Caro Amico had no competition. It was Portland's pizza place, and dear friends made it a popular family restaurant (there was also a full Italian menu), as well as a gathering place on the outskirts of downtown.

After her father died some years ago, Elsie's brother Kenneth took over until he too died in 1994. By then, Elsie, who had been a psychology major at Lewis & Clark College and a practicing counselor and therapist, and who had assisted her brother as his health failed, took over the business.

By now Elsie's two grown sons and a daughter were living elsewhere, and her nephew, King Baker, was running a pizza restaurant that was started across town by Elsie's brother Jack.

At first reluctant to carry on the Caro Amico tradition, Elsie says she made a "conscious decision" to like the business, which she admits she loves today.

"When I came here I found that, with a little bit of effort, I could bring joy and pleasure to people's lives. We have a very devoted clientele. On Sundays it's families who come in, and there are a lot of people who come just to sit in the bar.

"The bar is very important," she says from the viewpoint of a professional psychological counselor. "Most people are very honest with a bartender," she adds, laughing, "but I never became one. On the farm, I made it a point not to learn how to milk a cow so I wouldn't have to help with the milking. Here, I never learned how to tend bar."

Her gentle and persistent smile tells you she wants you to think about it.

She is a most gracious and unobtrusive hostess, however, making guests feel at home by offering a menu of ample and basic Italian dishes that, along with its famous pizza, features soup from a recipe over forty years old.

"My employees tend to stay," Elsie says, "and they say I'm easygoing. Sometimes I think I'm too much so," Elsie confesses with a self-deprecating smile.

The Caro Amico is open from 5 to 11 p.m. each day except Monday; it offers weekly specials and Northwest beers on tap, along with a full bar.

More important, in a rapidly changing Portland it remains a touchstone, a place where, relievedly, and except for those lampshades, very little has changed.

Looking out across the river where Mt. Hood cuts a neat isoceles triangle up into a clear afternoon sky, Elsie reflects, "People are adamant when they say, 'Don't change! Don't change! If we want a fern bar we'll go to a fern bar!'

"I think I can live with that."

The Cheerful Tortoise

1939 S.W. 6th Ave.
503-224-3377

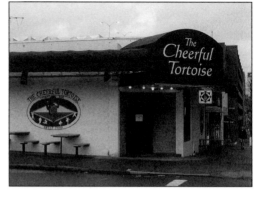

Crawling along for over forty-five years on the same corner near Portland State University, The Cheerful Tortoise has been slowly and steadily winning a race toward becoming what it started out to be years ago—a neighborhood tavern.

Once upon a time, when everyone was younger and drank more, the "Tortoise," as we knew it then, was a hangout for Portland State students and faculty; notably English majors and their professors who, after a hard day of wrestling with the dark side (is there any other?) of existentialism, would sink gratefully into the tavern's slingback chairs.

In those ancient and gentler days, when dinosaurs roamed the Park Blocks and PSU was still a college and an idea newly born, the Tortoise was a smaller, cozier place; only one corner where to sneak in after cutting class was a challenge well rewarded by putting you in the slow lane.

We all know Aesop's Fable—but to hell with catching up with the hare…

Now moved over into the fast lane, the Tortoise has rapidly gained on its long-eared adversary, offering a full hard liquor bar; a list of eighteen beers, foreign and domestic; a full menu that includes breakfast; pool tables; poker machines; and (weather permitting), under a bright new awning and facade, a sidewalk café.

Yet, to the relief of some of us oldtimers, the Tortoise has managed to retain a funky, undergraduate atmosphere that is compatible with what is now an incongrous hybrid of sports bar and Mexican café, yet still allowing an ambiance for, say, heavy discussions of Sartre and others of that ilk.

"This is as cozy as it gets," says Robert W. Jackson, Jr., the Tortoise's ebullient owner, who proudly proclaims the presence of eight (count 'em!) television sets that leap out at you from unexpected places, though the irrepressible Jackson adds with some restraint, "We're staying away from the big screens, however."

Exploring the Tortoise's dim and labyrinthine shell, one finds a cedar-shake-covered room adorned with sports jerseys and other mementoes, its center being a cone-shaped fireplace above which hang ships' lanterns, while to the rear the atmosphere segues through arches to a little bit of Santa Fe.

"It's a quality I like best," Jackson says enthusiastically, probably referring to the eclectica, but going on to explain how the corner is a kind of magnet for what he describes as "incredible foot traffic"—65% PSU students and faculty, and alumni like myself who once languished there often (and hopefully).

Weekend nights are big, and weekend mornings are smaller but a bit different with a breakfast crowd that is like the ambiance, the Tortoise having become a popular gathering place for customers who might once have been only tourists here.

The menu for all meals has a South of the Border accent, though good old reliable *norteamericano* standards are shuffled in: tuna, chicken and eggs-over mixed right in there with nachos, salsa and chimichangas.

And while some of us prefer to recall the Tortoise in its less frenetic, ambling, "to hell with the hare!" days, the energetic Jackson wants it known that this venerable tavern, now making a fast dash to success with its new running shoes on, is still a place where you can "eat, drink and have a quiet conversation."

Wearing a tee-shirt and cutting a grin that would lighten the heart of the most confirmed existentialist, Jackson emphasizes proudly, "Our motto is: 'No one has more fun than we do.' "

Somehow, you feel you ought to go along with a guy like that.

Cider Mill Restaurant & Lounge

6712 S.W. Capitol Highway
503-246-7266

Before suburbia this used to be all dairy farms around here, Swiss farmers and their contented cows perched on hilltops that roll gently against the backside of Portland's West Hills.

In those days, so long ago you don't want to remember, the Cider Mill was a real-life fruit and vegetable stand that sold the apple cider that gave the place its name.

The name lingers on, but, as it has been for several decades, the Cider Mill is a neighborhood tavern that still drags in its customers off a sharp curve in the road between Hillsdale and the village they now call Multnomah.

"I'd guess it's about eighty years old," says Ed Erickson, a retired Marine Corps gunnery sergeant who grew up down the street and has owned the tavern for the past eight years, "but nobody knows for sure."

Having grown up in the same neighborhood myself, and being the same age as Erickson, it's old home week for me. Ed's wife Peggy was graduated one year behind me at Lincoln High, and Ed, who went to Benson Tech, recalls how in the late 1940s and early '50s this was great terrain for kids to grow up.

"We raised a little hell, sure," Erickson reminds me, catching a view of Mt. Hood from a table in the Cider Mill's new outdoor beer garden. Then he chuckles, adding with a conspiratory wink, "but we couldn't do too much damage in those days, could we?"

It was mostly woods and farms around here then. You had to go into town to get into real trouble, "town" being pre-suburban Portland, a cozier, rosier and more compact place than it is now.

We take some time to reminisce, remembering street cars, electric railways, "dragging Broadway"—a weekend ritual for Portland teenagers—and how there used to be a movie theatre in Multnomah, a tiny place where, before they threw us out, all us "bad guys" sat up in the balcony and spit, smoked and swore.

Erickson's folks, Harold (whom everyone called "Swede") and Eva, once owned the now extinct "Dutch Tavern" in Hillsdale, a popular landmark recognized by its windmill.

Ed grew up in a little white house that still stands along Capitol Highway, just below the Mittelman Jewish Community Center, and first thing out of high school he went into the Corps. After leaving the Corps Erickson worked for a time in Saudi Arabia, but returned home when his webbed feet began to crack in the desert. He now lives in his folks' old place, and after 20 years of being in the Corps has no desire to move. These are his people around here.

Erickson tells how he got into the business, buying the Cider Mill from former owner Jim Demas "because," he admits flatly, "I couldn't get a job." Ed admits that when he took command the tavern, once described (unfairly) by a local newspaper columnist as "the sleaziest bar in town," was a bit run-down. "When I think about the condition it was in then," he says, "I guess the guy had a fair shot. Hell, when it rained we had to get buckets out."

Today, however, Erickson has the Cider Mill squared away. It's a clean, well-lit place with a new wood-paneled game room in back and a tiny meat-and-potatoes kitchen that serves entrées like chicken-fried steak, ribs, and its trademark "Friar Tuck Chicken," which is succulent despite the cholesterol. And a beer garden, of course, where on a sunny day oldtimers like Ed and myself can sit under an umbrella, listen to the commuter traffic and watch the new apartments making flank attacks on all sides.

"We've got a more diversified crowd now," he explains, "but still a lot of the old regulars. We also have a lot of younger people and they want all the action they can get, though I've shied away from live music. We've got a full-service restaurant (with a different specialty every day), a pool table, and I'm putting a horseshoe pit out here in the beer garden."

And business is good.

Erickson, a home-brew maker, acknowledges the popularity of local beers, and plans to open a microbrewery in a small building you can see over by the parking lot. Grinning above a gleaming white tee-shirt he got in Florida, he announces, "I want to see if I can make a good lager or Pilsener.

The label? "I'm going to call it 'Tuck's Beer,' " he says, "after the chicken."

Then he laughs, which he does infrequently.

On watch in his last duty station, in an old Southwest neighborhood where his past lives all around, Gunner Sgt. Ed Erickson, USMC-Ret., says he is a happy man. "Sure, it's a pain in the butt sometimes," he admits in a Corps dialect heavily spiced with salt, "but I wouldn't trade it for the world."

The Cider Mill is open every day of the week from 10 a.m. to 2 a.m.— except Christmas. "But I'm thinking about staying open on Christmas too," says Erickson, a well-traveled man who understands loneliness. "I've been there and I know. A lot of people have nowhere else to go."

Claudia's

3006 S.E. Hawthorne Blvd.
503-232-1744

Joe G. Bianco

Looking over, I see three young guys sitting around a table in the corner. They are drinking beer, watching television and yelling their heads off.

And why not? It's 2:17 on a drizzly Tuesday, and they're deep into a game between two obscure teams in the Women's International Soccer Association, Peru and Italy or something, someplace in the sun, and the women are running around and kicking the ball like crazy.

Hey! Who says Claudia's isn't a sports bar?

And not just any old sports bar, but a Portland original, going back to the post-Pleistocene days of 1957, when Claudia's was founded by Gene and Claudia (hence the name) Spathas as a "total concept" tavern—"warm," as it says on the menu, "friendly and physically and aesthetically pleasing."

Two years later, when I was just back from the Navy and spending more time in taverns than I should, the name "Claudia's" was murmured everywhere among hardcore tavern rats, evoking a new trend in Portland taverns. Not just another neighborhood tavern, Claudia's was a unique experience whose reputation made you feel it was the place you ought to be.

Today competition and trendier "concepts" have somewhat diminished Claudia's legendary uniqueness, with many young drinkers flocking to those places where the small ferns grow. Still, despite the intervening decades and a facelift, Claudia's feels much the same: a cozy place to eat, drink and cheer the ubiquitous sports contests that continue to dominate the tube—12 in all, including a rank of screens behind the bar, but who's counting?

One almost feels that an ill-timed request to watch "Oprah" or "Days of Our Lives" would result in immediate expulsion.

But perhaps not, for manager Martin Spathas, Gene's son, a mild-mannered guy of 30, explains that the place has mellowed a bit, reflecting what he calls the "granola-ish" transformation of Hawthorne Boulevard, now a burgeoning strip of boutiques and coffee houses.

Renovated out of its former funky grandeur several years ago, Claudia's now has four large pool tables, lottery games, a long bar facing a lineup of unusually comfortable high-backed stools, wood paneling, a fireplace, and an atmosphere vastly evolved from pure jock-frat-chug-a-lug chic.

Televised football, basketball and hockey games are the big crowd-gatherers, especially on weekends. But sweaty, loudmouthed, faded-glory jockstrappers have better manners than in the old days. "We used to get 180 Browns' fans in here," he says, "and it was weird. They would all get to barking at one time, drinking and raising hell. We don't see that much anymore," he adds gratefully.

It is obvious from his name that Spathas is Greek—"I know a few swear words is all," he admits—and along with sandwiches, including the heroic "Boss Burger," pizza, and other traditional fare, Claudia's features a few Greek specialties from old family recipes to tempt more exotic palates.

In addition to a full bar, Claudia's has 13 beers on tap, you can count at least 50 brands of bottled beers through the doors of the cooler, and, along with foreign and faraway domestic beers, labels from Northwest breweries and the new regional microbreweries are well represented.

And if you didn't know this was once the most popular sports bar in town, just look back behind the pool tables where a glass case contains some 200 trophies won by teams Claudia's has sponsored over the years, teams taverns used to field in the old, golden days of intramural competition. Now, however, Spathas explains, it's mostly tame stuff like darts and pool. There is less interest in tavern sports among customers, who tend to be not as loyal, nor as hard-drinking, as they used to be.

Spathas lives with his wife and two dogs just down the street, which, he says, is "convenient for emergencies." Though he puts in long hours, he loves the tavern, a family business that is open seven days a week.

Spathas says he arrived here, in his father's place, with a degree in sociology and other plans for his life, but now admits he wouldn't trade it for the world. "I've been working at Claudia's since I was knee high, and I love it," he says in his quiet way, echoing other longtime Portland barkeeps who often find themselves deep in love affairs with their bars and taverns.

Then he explains once more, "This has always been a sports bar, but it's a neighborhood bar as well. That's important. "

Business is good, Spathas admits, and somehow he finds it's still fun for him, "especially around four in the afternoon, when the regulars come in." Spathas smiles quietly and leans over like an old friend. "Yeah," he says, looking around, "sure, it's not like before. But I'd say Claudia's still has a good feel to it. And you know why? Listen," he says, pointing his finger straight up in the air, "when I go out of town you know what I look for? It's always for a place just like this."

Dad's Restaurant & Lounge

8608 N. Lombard St.
286-5512

Find Kenny Wilkinson hunkered down by the shady part of the bar, and he will tell you he has owned Dad's since 1958, tirelessly expanding the North Portland landmark that for decades has been the most popular drinking place in St. John's.

"You go across the St. John's Bridge, and there's Dad's," Wilkinson leaks out in a soft voice you can hardly hear.

"That's what people say."

I'll say.

Like the time my friend Dave, my best friend in grade school, walked into the bar barefoot, meeting me for the first time after an Army hitch in Korea. Dave, who has long since moved North, has always been a guy who sees light where the rest of us see dark and follows a drummer more distant than most of us can hear.

That night, Dave, who once had family around here, followed his drummer on a walk across the bridge, one of the most beautiful in the country—not on the sidewalk but on the graceful suspension cables far above—cables that loop up, and then down.

Then up again, where, if you have the guts and have had enough beer, you can look south and see the lights of downtown Portland, or, looking dizzily back down, pick out Dad's singing its sweet sirens' song on the corner.

Near that corner long ago was where I first met the late author Walt Morey, author of "Gentle Ben." Walt was the grand marshal of the St. John's Day Parade and was passing by in the back seat of an open convertible with a large but benign black bear who was pretending to be "Gentle Ben."

I stepped off the curb and said hello, and Walt growled hello back, right there beginning a friendship that endured for nearly thirty years.

Walt had spent his own time in St. John's, where as a young man he worked in a veneer plant with the late, great Western writer Louis L'Amour.

Once, after Louis was famous and I interviewed him through one long and delightful afternoon in a Portland hotel, he said to tell Walt "Howdy!" and that he was going to pay him back the ten bucks Walt had loaned him those many years past —which he did, just before Walt died.

In the old days Walt and Louis, both large, bear-like men, picked up spare cash in the boxing ring, fighting under assumed names in ham-and-eggers throughout the Northwest.

Since common labor and boxing are both thirsty work, I asked Louie if he'd ever been in Dad's, where anyone who has spent time in St. John's must have drunk at one time or another.

"Hell yes!" Louis said, and that was that.

But during that long afternoon I learned that Louie was liable to tell you anything if it sounded like a good story.

"Well, here's Dad's," Kenny counters, "still at the end of the bridge."

"That's right," says his diminuitive fourth wife, Gladys. "That's what the Portland Bridge Lady wrote in her book too: 'Here's Dad's.' "

Dark and vast, yet somehow cozy, Dad's has been owned by Wilkinson since 1958. In that time he has pushed back walls, lengthened the bar, added a restaurant and put up a lot of faded photographs on the walls, many of them Old St. John's when it was a city unto itself.

Back before the turn of the century the building was known as the the Cochran and Serber Saloon, explains Wilkinson, a man with a full head of hair who looks much younger than his 75 years, which seems rather remarkable for a saloon keeper with so many miles behind the bar.

"That old saloon was three stories high and there was a whorehouse upstairs," he says, beaking a sly grin and turning on his stool to point out a large fuzzy photograph of Cochran and Serber's, its balustrade festooned with somber-looking gents in derby hats.

As it was in the beginning, Dad's is still very much a working-class bar in a working-class neighborhood, and it's a relief not to find a suit, a fern or a bottle of Perrier water anywhere in sight.

In Dad's people drink a lot of beer and the music is country western. Then they drink more beer, maybe some whiskey, and from time to time wander over to talk to old friends in the restaurant or along the bar.

Men and women both; drinking, playing or just hanging out because Dad's is a friendly place where people know they must behave themselves. "You see that little woman?" Kenny asks, pointing over at Gladys. "She ain't big but she won't allow no trouble in here."

Wilkinson was six months old when his parents moved from Colorado to Willbridge, right across the river, and he was 11 when he walked across the St. John's Bridge on its opening day—June 13, 1931—wearing shoes and using the roadway, not the cables, by the way.

With start-up money he earned trucking scrap iron around town, Kenny got into the bar business. That was right after the Depression, and by 1960 he owned four bars, including the once infamous Lotus downtown (and which, I've found, seems to have been owned by everyone at one time or another).

But since St. John's is home, Kenny's heart has always been at Dad's, and Dad's, as Kenny and everyone around here knows, is the focal point of the community.

"Thursday nights we have cribbage," he begins. "Then there is bingo. . .also, the Optimists and Lions meet here, and. . ."

Wilkinson shakes his head and chuckles softly. "The place is a regular social club. Families come in for dinner and we have all kinds of parties for special occasions: birthdays, anniversaries, hirings, firings, or for community events like St. John's Days or Cinco de Mayo."

At the mention of Cinco de Mayo, the Mexican national holiday, Kenny begins praising a Mexican chef he has just hired.

"He's expensive but I like him. I eat the stuff myself," he confesses, laughing and patting a lean stomach. "It's damn good. I'm trying to get the food business up on a par with the booze."

Like the food, business is generally good, probably because the neighborhood seems to be always about the same.

"It hasn't changed much, I guess," Kenny offers. "We lost a couple of mills, maybe a cannery, is all."

His customers, mostly still ordinary hardworking folk, have changed very little as well.

"If anything," Kenny says, "people aren't as hard-drinking as they used to be. The tougher laws keep people from drinking and driving, and I think it's a good thing. A lot safer.

"One thing I really do miss, though, is the longshoremen. We don't get them much anymore. Those guys used to be here when I opened up in the morning, and before going to work they would sit at the bar and pour down whiskey and beer.

"But then the ships all started using containers and I lost a good part of my business. I really miss those longshoremen," he adds wistfully.

The most dramatic change, of course, has come with the simple passing of time, which Kenny accepts with stoic graciousness, convincing you that he's a happy man.

You hear it in his soft voice, and you see it in the way his eyes find Gladys, busy as ever, her small eyes keeping careful watch over the bar.

"Listen," he says clearly, "I've been in this business a long time, and it's still fun. When it isn't fun I won't do it anymore."

At Dad's; it's right there where it's always been, at the end of the St. John's Bridge.

Darcelle XV

208 N.W. 3rd Ave.
503-222-5338

"A pretty guy is like a melody…"

That's right, "guy" is the operative word here.

And if you just fell off the turnip truck believing in Santa Claus, the Easter Bunny and the veracity of professional wrestling, your response to the floor show at Darcelle XV might be one of bemused disbelief.

"Aw, come on, Gladys! You can't tell me that's a *guy* up there!"

"I'm telling you, Earl! You look close, he looks just like Manley Wiggins that runs the State Farm office back home."

"Well, I never seen Manley do nothing like that!"

Nor had I, certainly, until many years ago when a friend and I visited Finocchio's in San Francisco, our curiosities whetted by rumors of the nightclub's unique and naughty review featuring some of the world's most renowned female impersonators.

Newly discharged from the Navy, whose uniforms we still wore, we had arrived with our heterosexual courage afloat after an afternoon of draught beer; for it was the 1950s, after all, when "gay" was still defined in the traditional sense: "Showing or characterized by exuberance or mirthful excitement…"

Which, upon entering Finocchio's in a less than sober state and blearily eyeing the decked-out master (mistress?) of ceremonies, I displayed raucously, much to the chagrin of two huge men in civvies who braced me against a wall.

"Are you going to be good?" they queried, though not unkindly since they were obviously used to this sort of thing.

I was, I replied meekly, my head bobbing affirmatively as my toes were returned to the floor.

And so was the show, a glittering extravaganza of clever humor and elaborately costumed musical production numbers that would have delighted Flo Ziegfeld, and had us fooled from the start.

"If that's a guy up there," I said to my old shipmate Charlie as we watched a "person" strip down to a G-string, "I'll eat my white hat."

So now, jaded by time, and my white hat still uneaten, I sit in Darcelle's and catch a whiff of *déjà vu*, enjoying a show that, in one form or another, has been a landmark of offbeat Portland entertainment for the past thirty years.

Here, on a tiny stage in a small nightclub in Portland's Old Town, reality gives way to illusion as the house lights dim and a bevy of masculine beauties known as "Darcelle & Co." drag their stuff through what can only be described as a "class act."

Led by their durable impresario and namesake, Darcelle (who is actually the club's co-owner, Walter Cole) and in lavishly staged production numbers choreographed by his partner, Roc ("Roxy" to you) Neuhardt, the glittering ensemble appears two shows a night, four nights a week, in a phantasmagorical display of delightfully outrageous transvestism.

Or whatever.

Darcelle's is a demi-monde gaudily disguised: false eyelashes that go on forever, false nails, "falsies" that hide or enhance the inner man; gowns glittering with the gaudiness of rhinestones, bodies dripping with a king's ransom in ersatz family jewels…

Try to remember, these are guys under all that pancake makeup. You want Snow White, go to to Disneyland.

Yet once you begin to tolerate the gasping incredulity of the tourists around you (how did they find this place? you wonder), and begin to accept Darcelle's for what it is, you find yourself swept up in what is essentially a slick, good-natured spoof.

Suddenly Darcelle's has become its own "Magic Kingdom"—or "Magic Queendom," if you prefer.

"My theory is we're just actors playing a role on stage," explains Neuhardt, a bouncy blithe spirit who seems much younger than his 60 years. "What's important is how we look on stage, which doesn't necessarily represent our lifetyle."

Neuhardt and Cole, however, partners since 1967, who share a big old antique-filled home in Northeast Portland, are admittedly gay, as is their small cast, who for the most part are Portland-based entertainers.

Cole, who when out of drag is a youngish, blondish man of 65, is a native of Portland, a graduate of Lincoln High School who has spent the bulk of his career in local theater.

As Roxy explains, Cole acquired his sobriquet, Darcelle XV, in 1973 after winning the title of "Empress" during the XVth annual "Royal Court Games," a celebration that each year crowns an outstanding drag queen from among Portland's gay bars.

The regal name was subsequently given to the nightclub, which before that had been a popular "gay hangout," as Cole describes it, known as Demi's Tavern.

Presented at Darcelle XV today is not only a knock-'em-dead, dragged-out variety show featuring polished entertainers, but also a semi-seedy ambiance of nightclub kitsch just waiting for a film treatment by, say, Martin Scorsese or Gus Van Sant.

Walls are black matte, fabrics are animal skin knockoffs—tigers, leopards and such—tables are tight and dinky, while the walls are festooned with large glossy mug shots of entertainers, honored guests and friends, in or out of drag, whose autographs attest to Darcelle's infamy nationwide.

Put it all together around Darcelle's minuscule stage and tiny bar, and you have an atmosphere of light-hearted decadence to excite all but the most jaded lounge lizard.

In addition to the review, two complete shows each evening by Darcelle and Co. ($8), the club features a dinner-show package, but only prior to the first show, from 5 to 7 p.m.

Dinner currently is an offering of four rather uninspiring entrées reminding you that, at Darcelle XV, "the show's the thing."

And as Roxy reminds you with a light wiggle of his ringed fingers, "We started as a gay hangout, but we're not a 'hangout' anymore."

Roxy is a dancer whose life began, of all places, in the rough and ready community of West Yellowstone, Montana, a small hunting and fishing outpost on the western edge of Yellowstone Park.

Since then Roxy has been around. He made it to Hollywood for a while, was a chorus boy in Las Vegas; later he produced comedy numbers and landed in Portland where he did an acrobatic adagio act in Gracie Hanson's legendary (and sorely missed) "Roaring '20s Room" in the now-defunct Hoyt Hotel.

Gracie became his mentor, and through her he became involved in the local club scene, eventually pairing with Cole back in the late '60s.

"I always wanted to be an entertainer," Roxy explains. "But I thought I'd be Fred Astaire; I didn't think I'd end up being Ginger Rogers."

Cole, less animated off stage than his partner, sits quietly and explains how Darcelle's, along with the venerable Finocchio's, is unique on the West Coast in providing entertainment of this kind.

"Once there were more clubs doing this sort of thing," Cole says, "but nightclubs have disappeared as well. Now, on the West Coast there's just us and Finoccio's featuring talented female impersonators in full production numbers."

Popular among Portlanders, the club has an influx of tourists who drop by as well, mostly in the summer, Cole says, and some who return year after year from all over the country and even from overseas.

This can be attributed partly to a continual upgrading of the Old Town district, the former heart of Portland's once extensive and menacing skid road, which now includes a revived Chinatown (once the second largest in the country), a popular Saturday Market, as well as a proliferation of distinctive shops, boutiques, restaurants and bars served by light rail.

Darcelle's has played no small part in the district's recovery, and Cole and Neuhardt are leaders in Old Town's efforts toward regeneration.

"What we do is still flourishing," Cole says, referring to history. "This is part of a tradition that goes back to 16th century England (Shakespeare had boys playing women's roles), when cross-dressing was popular among the royalty.

"You might say we are 'royals' in our appetites," he adds playfully. "And we're not alone in our enjoyment of this kind of entertainment. The business is growing and continues to grow each year."

Graciously, Roxy attributes Darcelle's success to his partner.

"Walter is a master at moving audiences," he says with loving deference, since he plays no small part in developing and performing in their shows. "He's always been a character."

"When I'm Darcelle," Cole interjects, "I can do or say anything. I go with a kick on stage."

By getting a kick out of what they do, Cole and Neuhardt have become polished satirists who provide a naughty sendup of boys in girls' dresses, and they do it well.

They also do it with such good-natured panache that Aunt Gladys and Uncle Earl might return home to tell Manley Wiggins that he looks quite good in rhinestones after all.

Elephant & Castle

439 S.W. 2nd Ave.
503-222-5698

Back in the bad old days, when Shanghaiied sailors spread Portland's reputation as the most notorious port on the coast, the city also had the second largest Chinatown (after San Francisco) in the United States. At its peak Portland's Chinatown stretched for many blocks south of Burnside Street, with buildings along the way renovated to reflect the assimilated culture of their Oriental inhabitants.

While most have disappeared, the Waldo Building (built in 1886 by Judge John B. Waldo, an Oregon Supreme Court justice) remains on the corner of Southwest Second and Washington Street, where for over 30 years it has been home to the distinctive, popular Elephant & Castle pub.

Inside, vestiges of the past linger behind the Waldo's Victorian Italianate cast-iron architecture; shadowy reminders of the building's once infamous past as headquarters for a Chinese tong involved in opium, gambling and other illegal activities (its basement tunnels were used by crimps to move Shanghaiied sailors, or by the Chinese to make hasty retreats during raids).

"There's still a bench down there that was part of the old opium den," says Sharon Frederici, the Elephant & Castle's manager, "along with some wooden steps built back in the 1880s." Sharon pulls out a packet of photos, taken on one of her unofficial basement tours, that show not only remnants of the opium den but also the sealed-off entrances to the building's five tunnels—three headed south into what was old Chinatown, two aimed east toward the river, and one west, or uptown.

In the days when saloon keepers like Bunco Kelly were making a good income supplying sailing-ship captains with crews (sailors preferred the better conditions aboard the new steamships), hapless victims were slipped a Mickey Finn and held by crimps in cages under the streets. Portland had no seawall then, and tunnels led directly from riverside basements into hatchways for loading ship's cargo. Many an unfortunate sailor awoke to find himself at sea, with a splitting headache, and at the mercy of a cruel captain.

No sailors leave the Elephant & Castle through its basement these days, though the rich, slightly worn *fin de siècle* ambiance implies the possibility.

When I was a young reporter in the old "Two and Oak" Police Headquarters down the street, darts was the Elephant's game. On most nights the pub's several boards would be crowded with men, some playing at being British, others who truly were. (Portland, on the same latitude, can be a lot like London, especially on dark, rainy nights murky with fog. Then the Elephant becomes an appropriate haunt for Anglophiles, who burrow into its comfortable gloom, call for a pint and order up the house specialty: fish and chips.) "Our fish and chips have an international reputation," Sharon says proudly. A sturdy woman, she can be imagined serving ale to Falstaff's mates in *Henry V*.

The Elephant & Castle's name comes down from Shakespeare's time, a period when 16th-century Spain was Europe's dominant power. During that time a Spanish noblewoman, the Infanta de Castilla, on her way to London to be married, stopped overnight in the village of Southwark. Unable to pronounce her title, villagers referred to her as "the Elephant and Castle." In later years the symbol of an elephant with a castle on its back became the hallmark for Southwark's knifemakers. When the knifemakers relocated in the 18th century the site was taken over by a pub, "The Elephant & Castle," famous in London to this day.

You see, it's that kind of place. Walls are darkly paneled; flags of Great Britain and its former colonies are draped above a worn bar. Sharon points out three genuine Tiffany lamps overhead, as well as a massive chandelier and other bibelots…and, oh yes, dartboards. "It's not like it used to be, though," Sharon says. "We have league play on Thursday nights and that's about it."

Sharon's mother, Hildreth "Hillie" Frederici, the proprietor, sitting nearby, agrees. "It's not like it used to be back in the old days. People don't hang around downtown like they used to. Everybody's in such a hurry."

Leaning over, Sharon nods. "Yeah, business has been heck of a lot better. We sell a lot of food—our food's real good—and we get a lot of gamblers now coming in for the lottery games. But they're a good, well-behaved crowd, and we get a lot of people for lunch and dinner."

The Elephant has a full bar, a lot of good tap beers, and an impressive menu featuring traditional British pub food: shepherd's pie, steak and mushroom pie, bangers, ploughman's lunch, liver and onions, along with assorted salads, sandwiches, burgers, soup and seafood.

More important, perhaps, is the Elephant & Castle's history. A designated Portland landmark, it's the first building you see coming off the Morrison Bridge into downtown, and its presence, the bold Elephant & Castle logo on its facade, is a most appropriate introduction to Old Town—when Portland was bad, back in the good old days.

Goose Hollow Inn

1927 S.W. Jefferson St.
503-228-7010

Not alone in her obsessive hatred for Bud Clark's Goose Hollow Inn—"The Goose," as it is known to its denizens—was the wife of a former friend of mine who, desperate to reclaim her husband from the Goose's cozy nest, threatened more than once to "burn the damn place down!"

"It's the only way I'll get him to stay home," she lamented. "He loves that tavern more than me and the kids."

It was that kind of place once—and perhaps still is. The Goose's honk is an irresistible siren's song to husbands (and some wives) lured all too frequently into its warm and downy embrace. To others The Goose was simply home. The late legendary Max Berg, disgruntled journalist and resident curmudgeon, had his mail delivered there, while a small, tenacious group of men seemed affixed to the bar in a permanent tableau.

For me in those halcyon days before booze had become my personal adversary, Bud Clark's famous Budweiser Beer was a lubricant to dreams and conversation, while Clark himself, a congenial, bearded man who was Portland's mayor from 1985 to 1992, was a benevolent host concerned that his patrons not fight and get home safely.

Behind a matchbook cover proclaiming The Goose's dedication to good beer, food, music and "stimulating company" is printed this admonition: "We are also dedicated to extremes of opinion hoping that a liveable marriage will result. If physical violence is your nature either develop your verbal ability or leave."

Occasionally, Clark himself might encourage departure by inquiring tactfully, "Don't you have a home?" My reply in those days was often, "Yes, and I'm there."

A native Portlander, Clark is a health-conscious beer drinker who conducted his campaign for mayor aboard his bicycle and canoe, and while in office rode to City Hall on the bike he still rides all over town. At 63 he is a sturdy, Santa Clausian gent who favors lederhosen and reveals his grand sense of humor in a nationally infamous "Expose Yourself to Art" poster, a photograph featuring Clark whipping open a rumpled raincoat to a startled bronze statue (female) on Portland's Transit Mall.

Somewhat appropriately, Tri-Met's new westside light rail system will have a station on Southwest Jefferson opposite The Goose's front door.

The tavern, basically a large wooden shed, has changed very little since it was built as a fruit stand, Clark thinks about 1926. The former mayor made it The Goose in 1967, transforming it from a more languid venture, "Ann's Tavern," of years before.

But if you had fallen asleep in The Goose at its beginning, then got a wake-up call today, about all you would find different is the price of beer and wine, the availability of non-alcoholic beer (Max Berg may spin in his grave), and vegetarian items—"Gardenburgers, Rachel's Reuben: 'All the sauerkraut you can eat, $5.50' "—edged onto the menu by Clark's daughter while Dad was off being mayor.

In fact, to a sharing, caring, '90s kind of person who eschews real beer, wine and cigarettes, The Goose may actually be seen as a kind of health club for Portland beer and wine drinkers.

Goose "ambiance" (sorry, Max), is much like a house party, a gaggle of patrons varying between a hardcore of hard-drinking, hard-talking old-timers and a flock of younger, eager amateurs anxiously yearning to become habitués, while nibbling intensely on the periphery are "relationships" in various stages of conception, continuation or conflict.

"...So I met this chick at The Goose..." is an expression as familiar to Portlanders as "do you think it will rain?"

Once The Goose was a hangout for architects, artists, writers, politicians and others skilled in shooting the *caca de toro*. Today, however, while a few of the old cliques remain, there is a more eclectic mix of men and women moving between the bar, the window booths, the new deck outside and, in the back, at the heart of The Goose, the eternally murky "Fairfax Room."

Looking around a place that has changed imperceptibly in thirty years, Clark comments succinctly, "A lot of my friends have died."

Included with Berg among The Goose pantheon are award-winning journalist Bruce Baer, Jim Hicks, whose earphoned countenance looks down from a wall in the Fairfax Room, Clark's long-time good friend Charlie Raymond, a venerable bartender known to everyone as "Charlie Brown," and many others, good Clark friends for years, lost to time, disease, accident and life's harsher weather.

A tour of The Goose is a primer of Portland history, and Clark is a competent guide. Goose Hollow is named after the geese once raised here for market by women before the turn of the century, and the tavern's walls

History by the Glass

display photographs of the hollow taken by Olin K. Jeffrey in 1919. There are also some of Clark's own photographs, including one of him as a boy selling lemonade in his old Portland neighborhood.

If you can catch him in his busyness, Clark will tell you he opened his first tavern, the popular Spatenhaus, across from Civic Auditorium in 1961. The tavern was later removed to build the Ira Keller Fountain.

Clark will also tell you he still owns his first pizza oven, and claims the distinction of being the first guy in town to serve sandwiches prepared in a pizza oven, explaining how tavern food has improved since then.

At one time The Goose was pouring two hundred or more kegs of Budweiser beer a month, the highest volume of any tavern in the state, and Clark says, "I still pour a good glass of beer. I tell my people, 'put a good head on it.' " Though the flow of beer has been diminished somewhat by the temperance of the time, The Goose now offers on tap a broader, more select variety of brews that includes imports and a respectable number of labels from Oregon's renowned microbreweries.

The Goose also offers a modest but respectable selection of wines, wine coolers, soft drinks, fruit and vegetable juices, as well as sparkling water to wash down a tavern-deli menu of pizza, sandwiches, soup and salads.

Myth, legend and Portland tradition all blend in The Goose melting pot, where anyone can become easily addicted to the feel of the place. For myself and other oldtimers, The Goose is a place to go on a quiet Sunday afternoon when it's uncrowded and you can actually see the floor; especially in fall or winter, when a gray Portland sky drips down raindrops heavy as falling lead. Those are days when the ghosts come out…when you can imagine Max Berg grumbling and Charlie Brown working cheerfully at the bar; when, if you look closely, you might spot the angry wife of a long-gone friend sneaking up on The Goose with a determined look and a box of matches.

Helvetia Tavern

10275 N.W. Helvetia Rd.
Hillsboro, Ore.
503-647-5286

"Good ol' boy caps"—you know what they are: those ubiquitous, fit- any-size baseball caps whose peaks advertise everything from heavy equipment to chewing tobacco, while others proclaim their owners' personalities: "Instant asshole, just add beer," "Seagulls Overhead!" (with a suspicious white blotch), or one of my personal favorites, "Old Fart."…and hundreds more adages, proverbs and defiant *bons mot* expressing the proletarian state of mind. Caps like these adorn the ceiling of the Helvetia Tavern in relentless profusion, hanging bills-down and reminding you of multi-colored bats, over a barroom largely unchanged since the turn of the century.

In those days there were mostly Swiss dairy farmers around here (hence the name, Helvetia, which means "Little Swiss"), while today the softly rolling hills, sub-alpine woodland and meadows that endure are a bucolic Heidi's dream as you stand in the parking lot and gaze west.

"Some of the regulars were angry when we paved the lot," comments owner Cindy Harrah, "but with the crowds we really had no choice—and the county made us do it."

The crowds are mostly flatlanders who swoop up from the valley floor; from Portland (15 miles away), Hillsboro, Beaverton and other places. Regulars come in too, with their good ol' boy caps, bending their knees against a worn wooden bar upholstered with burlap bags whose labels reveal they once held Northwest spuds. Although the view alone is worth the climb up old Helvetia Road, customers come for the famous "Jumbo Burger," a full half-pound in a six-inch bun—and you take it the way it comes. A sign on the wall warns: "This is not Burger King. You don't get it *your* way. You take it *my* way or you don't get the son of a bitch!" Other signs suggest with rural subtlety that you "go bite yourself in the ass!," or remind gently, "farting prohibited!"

"This is a place with character," says Cindy, an attractive 36-year-old who, with her now-ex-husband Andy Harrah, took over the Helvetia in 1979.

Since Andy's departure Cindy has run the tavern alone, helped by a staff of twelve who tend bar, wait on customers and (apparently) cook Jumbo Burgers any way they want. They also clean up, and every Easter, helped by locals and habitués, the staff closes the tavern and all hands muster to oil the well-worn wooden floors. "It's the only day other than Christmas that we're closed," Cindy says cheerfully. Regular hours are 11 a.m. to 10 p.m., Sunday to Thursday, and 11 a.m. to 11 p.m. on Friday and Saturday.

The Helvetia offers a modest menu tucked right beside the napkin dispenser. Listed along with burgers are turkey, ham and grilled cheese sandwiches, "Garden Burgers," halibut fish and chips and other items. The Helvetia serves beer and wine, with Oregon microbreweries and vineyards well represented—including a new pinot noir from nearby Helvetia Vineyards, owned by present Oregon Congresswoman Elizabeth Furse.

Arriving on a bright sunny day, you find the tavern to be a cozy anachronism, but with some history. We already know the Swiss were here, but we are perhaps unaware of how the tavern evolved from an early building constructed in 1910 as a meeting hall and general store. After that place burned in 1918, the store was rebuilt by one John Wanger, who added gas pumps in the 1920s, while John's dad, "Pop" Wanger, built a small, shed-like poolhall alongside.

In those days electric trolleys and trains ran through the community, but beer didn't get back on the track until Prohibition pulled out of the station in 1933. By 1941, however, the Helvetia had become a full-fledged tavern, according to Vicki Baskk, whose grandparents once owned the place. Vicki, in her handwritten family history, recalls lively, accordion-pumped dances in a rebuilt hall across the street, a place that up until 1973 was used for weddings and other social events. "This was a very popular place to be on the weekends," Baskk writes, just as it is today.

Looking out past the Helvetia's beer garden at a natural landscape that seems to go on forever, Cindy expresses her fondness for the tavern she's acquired. "I've come to love it, and my customers," she says, sneaking a grin. "Hey, this is just a funky old place in the country and I'm always happy here." Cindy, who has two young children, has worked to maintain the tavern's social role within the hillside community. Among other things she helps support Helvetia's baseball team and boys' club. "This isn't like the tavern business," she says. "This is a real community and the benefits go both ways."

On Wednesday nights there is bingo, and lucky winners take home plastic pink flamingoes or sacks of birdseed. The crowd at different times may include families, kids, business people, golfers, motorcyclists (the good kind), or people on their way to or from the Coast.

"That's another thing I like," Cindy adds. "We get so many different kinds of people. You just can't predict who may come in here."

Asked about the future, Cindy breaks a grin as broad and bright as a country sunrise. "I like it the way it is," she says.

History by the Glass

The Horse Brass Pub

4534 S.E. Belmont St.
503-232-2202

Tall, thin and somewhat tattered around the edges, his red-rimmed eyes peering from beneath shoulder-length hair, Don Younger looks like a man who just spent the night in the back seat of a 1966 Chevrolet.

After lighting a Camel and blowing a puff into the cool dark coziness of The Horse Brass Pub, Younger hunkers down to confess, "Listen, I'm just an old tavern rat, and I always will be."

This is not a surprise after a first glimpse at the man, but a seeming incongruity when you get to know Younger and see how his personality has transformed the Horse Brass into a finely detailed replica of a comfortable English pub.

At 54 Younger, who has owned the pub since 1976, is an admitted Anglophile with a romantic's penchant for collecting things. His pub is festooned with the trappings of empire, creating an atmosphere so authentically British that sojourners from Picadilly often claim they feel at home here.

As Younger explains between puffs, "Something just clicked. In fact, when I started out I had only a fantasy of what an English pub should be. But then I decided to make it the best pub there is.

"Then the 'Brits' started coming in, and I've heard them say, 'We're stunned. This is the best English pub we've been in.' "

Outside of Britain, of course.

Yet, a dozen or so visits to the British Isles over the years have confirmed Younger's vision of what a pub should be. The Horse Brass evokes a venerable Victorian quality, a Dickensian ambiance appropriate to meetings of the Pickwick Club, retired members of an RAF squadron, or thirsty bowlers and batters just off the cricket pitch.

The pub is dimly lighted beneath a low, heavy-beamed ceiling, while glimpses of the outside 20th century are viewed through small-paned windows recalling centuries past. Walls are hung with flags, photographs and signs recalling Britain's fading imperial splendor; maps near the kitchen guide you through London's streets and subways, while polished horse brass medallions gleam around a bar glittering with glasses and bottles, the bar being a snug place where a thicket of wooden tap handles are pulled beneath an antique sign that reads, simply, "Public Bar."

Quite prominently, there is a gnarly, highly polished Irish shillelagh hanging over the bar as well.

"Whenever I was in England," Younger says, "whatever I saw for sale in antique stores, pubs or whatever, if I liked the feel of it I'd grab it."

And since the Horse Brass is an authentic, self-respecting pub, dart boards are targeted on the walls to be thunked by amateurs, and by those members of teams Younger has sponsored through the years.

After beginning as a tavern with only vague aspirations to becoming a pub, the Horse Brass today offers not only beer, wine and a respectable hard liquor bar (with an impressive selection of single-malt whiskys) but a restaurant as well.

Snapping his Zippo on another Camel ("This is a pub, not a hospital," Younger says defiantly), Younger passes over a broad menu laden with "British Specialities": bangers, pasties, Scotch eggs, steak and kidney pie, a ploughman's lunch, fish and chips; as well as colonial fare: burgers, chicken, salad and sandwiches, and a light list of heavy desserts to fuel an evening of darts (provided by the management).

Younger confesses drily, "When I started out, I thought food was chips behind the bar, and I considered hard liquor a condiment. Now I'm a restaurant," he says, as if he still can't believe it. "And we're serving more food now. Some of the food we have now—even I can't believe it. It's fantastic."

Not that beer is ignored, certainly, for the Horse Brass taps pull down 29 beers and ales from several continents, including a full contingent from the Northwest's fine microbreweries, and there is a vast array of bottled foreign and domestic beers as well.

Lighting another Camel, the old tavern rat says proudly, "I'm held in high regard among the microbrewing community. Our microbreweries have made Portland 'Beer City,'" he boasts almost gleefully, before telling about how the pub has been written up in several national magazines.

"I'm amazed when people come in and say, 'I've heard so much about you.' They come from all over, and are curious why Portland has the biggest and best selection of local beers in the country."

Flipping quickly through pages of his memory, Younger gets that wily old tavern rat look, lights another Camel and says, "You know, up until twenty years ago (a period he calls "the dark ages") this was a 'Blitz' and 'Oly' (Olympia) town. Now it's become an incredible drinking town."

Grinning, he stops to recite an archaic bit of doggerel: " 'Oly is holy, ignorance is Blitz,' is what we used to say," before chuckling like a man who can't believe things have gone so far.

Like Younger himself, a graduate of Grant High who, after a short stint at Portland State College, where he "majored in bridge and minored in pinochle," worked as an office manager for Lever Brothers before being enticed into the tavern business by his brother Bill.

"Bill came home from Vietnam and said, 'Why don't we get a tavern?' He wasn't into the tavern scene like I was, and I told him, 'Hell, I don't want to own a tavern. I'm having too much fun drinking in them.'

"Then Lever Brothers transferred me to L.A., and I looked around and said, 'I don't ever want to live in this goddamned place!' I came back and Bill and I opened the Mad Hatter. That was a good old workingman's tavern that is now the Bear Paw Inn, over on Milwaukie Avenue. I also owned Strawberry Fields, out in Gresham, before I got into this place."

Younger bought the Horse Brass from two partners with the same first name, Jay Brandon and Jay Kileen, and gives them credit for setting up business off of what Younger refers to as "the drinkers' trail."

"At first the locale was a drawback," Younger admits, "but now we're near an area that has become trendy (Southeast Hawthorne Boulevard), and in a neighborhood that was once fighting for its life. It's still transitional," he adds, "but we're getting the yuppies calmed down a bit."

By word of mouth, through magazine stories and, more recently, computer internet, the Horse Brass attracts customers of all kinds from everywhere; a clientele the much-experienced Younger describes as "normal people."

"It's not cool anymore to get drunk and raise hell in taverns like we used to," he says, grinning at the memory. "People don't drink as much and are looking for something more. And being established I don't have to prove anything to my customers or myself. I get people in from New York City who say the place is incredible. They appreciate the warmth and say they feel like they're among family.

"Hey, I don't advertise, people just find us. We're more well known than you can imagine. I can't bring in the customers; my job is just to reward them when they come here."

As any serious old tavern rat worth his beer nuts should, Younger has followed the transformation of Portland taverns from basic hardcore neighborhood hangouts to what he considers higher quality, "grownup" places, largely through the easing of Oregon's once much tougher liquor laws.

"I remember when you couldn't sing, dance, have live music or serve wine in taverns, which in the old days closed at 1 a.m.," Younger says.

"But those days are gone. When wine came in we could stay open later, more women came in and soon everyone was singing and dancing. You might say the big breakthrough was 'wine, women and song.' "

Younger attributes the increased sales of imported beers, which took off back in the 1970s, and the subsequent growth of microbreweries, to the more discriminating palates of women drinkers.

"Women were an easy sell for the more exotic micros and imports. They'd come in, take a sip and say, 'This isn't beer, this is good!' "

Inescapably, however, Horse Brass customers are attracted by the pub's nostaglic atmosphere, symbolized by a sad-eyed drawing (by James Macko) of Portland jazz great Monte Ballou, leader of the legendary "Castle Jazz Band."

While Younger explains the drawing on the wall, titled "The Ghost of Monte Ballou," and points to Ballou's Oregon license plate, "JAZZ-4U," hanging nearby, he says, "You might say Monte died here. He would come in and play during his last years, and…well," he says softly, "I loved that old man."

Former mayor and fellow tavern owner Bud Clark campaigned here, as did the now infamous former Oregon Senator Bob Packwood, among others.

"Packwood came in often, and he was a good customer," Younger says. "But," he adds almost wistfully, "I suppose now I won't be seeing him for a while."

While newer Portland taverns, pubs and drinking places come and go, Younger says the Horse Brass keeps getting better every year, a continuing success he attributes to a "holy trinity" of management, "dynamite" employees, and loyal customers who feel at home here.

"It's just an honest bar, one big family where people can come in and feel comfortable. There is an incredible feeling of warmth, and I've never had any trouble," he adds. "I love this place. I never get tired of it. If I'm in town I'm here."

And, of course, it is Younger's long and loving devotion to taverns that has made the Horse Brass the success it is today.

Stretching out in flannel shirt and jeans, Younger seems part of the furniture, an old tavern rat who says, "I can't tell you or write it out for you; there's no formula, just an instinct that takes over. My job is to interpret the bar and know what goes into it."

Then he lights another Camel, looks around lovingly and admits, "You have to love it or lose it. Mentally it can eat you alive. I'm just an old beer-drinking guy, and my heart's in a good old tavern. Give me a good old tavern with a shuffleboard, a jukebox and a bottle of Henry's, and I'm in heaven."

Kight Photography

History by the Glass

Huber's

411 S.W. Third Ave.
503-228-5686

Joe G. Bianco

Walk into Portland's oldest restaurant any time of day and it's always 1910, the dark mahogany paneling, brass fittings and ethereal stained-glass skylight of Huber's restaurant evoking ghosts of the city's romantic past.

With its decor virtually intact since moving into the heart of the Railway Exchange Building (now the Oregon Pioneer Building) in the century's first decade, Huber's keeps its menu intact as well, still featuring its legendary roast turkey, a specialty since Huber's began as the Bureau Saloon back in 1879.

That was at the corner of Southwest First Avenue and Morrison Street, when its proprietor was W. L. Lightner, a man who unwittingly changed destiny by hiring Frank R. Huber, a remarkably dapper gent, as his bartender back in 1884.

Three years later the impeccable Mr. Huber became a partner, and by 1888 he was sole owner of the saloon, which in 1895 changed both its name and address, becoming "Huber's" at 281 S.W. Washington St.

Several years before, however, in 1891, the restaurant was assured of its legacy when Huber hired as chef a young Chinese immigrant by the name of Jim Louie.

Louie had left China when he was eleven years old, stowing away aboard a sailing ship and arriving in Portland in 1881, when the West Coast was home to thousands of immigrants from Louie's native province of Canton.

Louie was the great-uncle of the present owners, Jim, David and Lucille Louie, and after his arrival had apprenticed to a French woman who owned a local bakery. Soon after, he was working in the old Peerless Saloon on Alder Street when Huber, learning of his culinary skills, enticed him into his establishment.

During the great flood of 1894, Louie became a legend when he served steamed clams and turkey sandwiches from a rowboat floating inside the saloon.

The legend endured, and in later years Louie's turkey sandwiches and his succulent coleslaw, another house specialty, made the saloon a favorite establishment of Portland businessmen who still lunch there today.

When Huber died in 1912, Louie became the manager for Mrs. Huber, cooking turkeys and serving cocktails over the bar with the same dignity and meticulous care of his late benefactor.

When Prohibition decimated many of Portland's famous old saloons, Louie and Mrs. Huber planned to close the bar. But at the insistence of their customers they transformed the saloon into a fine restaurant, augmenting its specialties with a broader dinner menu featuring steaks, chops and a variety of Northwest seafood.

To keep up with the trade, Louie hired a staff of Orientals, and by 1939 the restaurant had gained a national reputation. In 1940, following the death of Mrs. Huber, Louie formed a partnership with her son John.

Jim Louie eventually became the sole owner, and in 1946, after working a full day, he died in the restaurant that he loved.

An oil painting of Louie in his distinctive chef's hat and carving a perfectly browned turkey hangs prominently in Huber's dining room.

A primer of Huber's long history is a required appetizer for new patrons or those native Portlanders like myself who, through time, had lost track of the restaurant where many of us had our first "restaurant meal."

Huber's has been designated as a Portland historical landmark and is listed on the National Registry of Historic Places, and looking around you can easily see why. Beneath its distinctive skylight, highlighting the well-polished paneling and thick columns of Philippine mahogany, are the very same tables and booths intact on its gleaming, original terrazzo floor.

Lingering from the old days too are the brass cash register behind the bar, a brass ship's clock above the door and the pewter wine bucket on its silver stand.

In this time vanishing atmosphere you can imagine a Portland visit from the spirits of Dorothy Parker and Robert Benchley, exchanging well-lubricated witticisms in one of Huber's deep, dark booths.

James Louie, namesake and grand-nephew of Jim, who manages the restaurant with his brother David and sister Lucille, would have it so. Louie took over from his father Andrew (an original Jim Louie nephew), who died in 1989, and is intent on maintaining Huber's tradition into a second century.

A dapper, well-turned out man of 49 whose sartorial elegance would have made old man Huber proud, Jim began working in the restaurant when he was a freshman at Portland's Benson High School.

Though he studied for a time at Portland State University, he finally succumbed to his ancestral birthright and has accepted the restaurant as his legacy.

His heart was apparently in the right place, for Jim Louie's descendants have brought about a remarkable revival of Huber's, not only enhancing the menu, but polishing up its bar so that once again it has become one of the most popular and fashionable watering holes in town.

By maintaining his deep love for its history and tradition, and having inherited his family's proprietorial skills, the present Jim Louie lighted a fire under Huber's when he began concocting his now-famous Spanish coffees, served to customers with fiery panache.

Louie torched his first Spanish coffee in 1975, igniting a fad among a young, trendy and enthusiastic downtown clientele whose inordinate fondness for the flaming cocktail has helped Huber's set a record for the most Kahlúa sold in any bar in the United States.

"The Kahlúa people told us that themselves," Louie, a rapier-thin man who greets his guests in a spiffy tuxedo, says proudly.

"We use a case a day on weekdays, and average two cases a day on weekends," he explains, apropos of the good businessman he is.

Huber's also has a full bar with a selection of beers from Northwest microbreweries, and its wine list gives priority to Northwest labels, all of which are suggested to accompany menu entrées.

In fact, despite Huber's famed popularity as an eatery, Louie will tell you drinks served from its mirrored bar claim a full sixty percent of his business.

"Downtown Portland is getting healthy again," he claims enthusiastically. "Light rail is bringing people back; we have the 'Schnitz' (Arlene Schnitzer Concert Hall in the Performing Arts Center), the auditorium, movies, as well as a lot of other new drinking places and an influx of small, upscale hotels in the downtown core."

Huber's is open 11 a.m. to midnight, Monday to Thursday, noon to 1 a.m. Friday and Saturday; but, as you might expect, Friday nights are the busiest, often standing room only with after-work crowds chattering gaily around Huber's tiny tables, ablaze with coffee, cognac and Kahlúa.

To stand on line in the hallway outside, which is lined with photographs of Old Portland, peering in at Huber's happy customers and anticipating what awaits within, can be a pleasant experience in itself.

Fortunately for those who haven't yet discovered this wonderfully preserved, turn-of-the-century restaurant and bar, Louie has no plans to change, and intends keeping Huber's the same as it was back in 1910.

"No, no, no!" he insists placatingly beneath the painting of his honored namesake, whose spirit continues to dominate the room.

"We intend to keep the place intact. All I want is to bring gratification and joy to our guests."

Personally, I like to experience Huber's in the way old Portlanders have throughout the century; by dropping by on a long, gray, rainy afternoon when time seems suspended and the past gathers tightly around you: 1910 once again, and the way it always will be.

The Hutch

4606 N.E. Glisan St.
503-235-4729

Now this is more like it!

Reassemble The Hutch inside the Smithsonian Institution, and you could label the exhibit, "A Good Old Portland Tavern, The Way It Used to Be."

Enter this quiet, smoky time warp from the 1950s, and if you are of a certain age, you sigh, settle in and say to yourself, "I'm home again! Safe in a place free of ferns, fresh air and the frustrations of 'feminine mystique.' "

Order a glass of beer, maybe some Beer Nuts...what the hell!...light up a Camel straight; no one gives a damn.

Then look around.

It all comes back, doesn't it? Good friends and neighbors laughing above a jukebox that's too loud, beneath a profusion of dancing beer signs (Remember the Hamm's Bear?); playing pool in the back, while in the front...my God! Is that a shuffleboard table?

Hey...! Does a Hamm's Bear go in the woods?

There, in all its polished hardwood magnificence, stretched along one wall in anachronistic grandeur, the former king of all tavern games, rare now as a Columbia River salmon.

Listening to the soft click of the shuffleboard pucks, you remember when taverns had them everywhere; when shuffleboard actually defined a tavern and there were vast and dramatic tournaments that saw men and women jousting for trophies across the waxed maple boards; before television, pool tables and video poker drove shuffleboard into hiding, leaving the game to languish in a few nostalgic places like The Hutch.

"Yeah, I know. I still love the game too," says Dennis Espe, who with his wife Linda and a partner, Jim Salmon, has owned The Hutch since 1976.

"I can remember all the tournaments around town," he says, watching a handful of mailmen having a good time on the board. "I used to play all over. I once knew a one-armed guy who beat everybody, playing both sides of the board with one hand. I remember…"

And Espe goes on like this for a while, off in some memories; a 55-year-old, normal-looking, soft-spoken guy who grew up just down the street and still lives in the old neighborhood.

"My dad used to bring me up here," he says, recalling the days when kids could go into taverns with their parent. "He used to sit me at the bar, then have a couple of beers. This has always been a good neighborhood. We've got the sons and daughters of parents who used to come in here—who still come in here!

"Hell, this was my watering hole," Espe confesses expansively, waving his arms around the L-shaped tavern and over his shoulder, saying hello to a guy named "Al."

(Just like there are no bald winos, in taverns there is always a guy named Al.)

A graduate of Laurelhurst Grade School and Grant High, Espe is a veteran of Navy's elite Submarine Service whose strict requirements of a cool head and steady nerves are appropriate for anyone owning a tavern.

His partner, Jim Salmon ("Just like the fish," Espe says), is a retired Navy chief.

"We run a pretty tight ship," Espe says. "No trouble, no fights."

As have a lot of tavern owners, Espe ended up in the business unexpectedly, arriving at The Hutch weary of life's mainstream career highways.

"I once worked in the mail room at *The Oregonian*," he confesses, "then I went to work for Fred Meyer. I worked for Freddy for years, moving up to assistant manager. Then one day I was working at a checkstand and it just dawned on me. I said to myself, 'I can't take this crap anymore.' I wanted to do something for myself before it was too late; I wanted a job where I wasn't always pissed off at someone else."

So one day while Espe was drinking in The Hutch, the former owner, Prescott Hutchins, asked him if he wanted to be a partner.

"Prescott was almost like a dad to me," Espe says fondly. "He was a retired Portland Police detective and had been an All-American football player at Oregon State. We became partners, and I eventually bought out his half in 1976."

Hutchins had given his name to the tavern, whose history begins somewhere in the late 1920s, Espe explains, when it was known as the "Laurelcrest Tavern," (as it still is to some of Espe's older customers).

Providence Hospital is located right across the street, and hospital employees have mingled for years with neighborhood denizens, many of whom walk to the corner tavern, which is open from 11 a.m. to 1 a.m., and every day but Thanksgiving and Christmas.

"We've got a mixed crowd in ages anywhere from 25 to 70," Espe says, "and I try to keep something going all the time. We have a Halloween party, barbecues, a picnic in the fall; there are pool and dart teams, I have two bowling teams, a co-ed softball team and a senior men's baseball team...That's for guys over 40," he adds after a significant pause.

"And, oh yes, bingo in the wintertime."

This particular New Year's Eve Espe will raffle off a 1979 Chevrolet Corvette, a ploy he qualifies by saying, "You have to do these little promotions. I've been at it so long, though, sometimes I get a little burned out, trying to do something different to keep things lively."

On the wall above the shuffleboard, still surrounded by mailmen, is a tee-shirt depicting two large floor safes in a compromising position. The caption reads, "Safe sex," and Espe cracks a comfortable grin that tells you he feels safe here as well.

"Do I like it? Yeah, sure I like it. I like the people and I know just about everybody by name. I even have my own 'Cliff the mailman,' like on 'Cheers.' He'll be in after a while."

Old customers come into The Hutch and find their beers waiting on the bar, and Espe says, "Yeah, I guess we pretty much spoil them. But it's like family, and this place feels pretty much like home to so many of my old customers. I even have people coming here I used to know in grade school.

"One time I even had a young couple who stopped by on the way to their wedding. A big limo pulls up outside and they run in all dressed up and sit down at the bar. They had a couple of pitchers, and when I asked what was going on, they said they needed 'reinforcement' before the ceremony."

In an alcove opposite the bar is a covey of lottery games, a concession to the times, but everywhere else is a random profusion of conventional tavern memorabilia that causes Espe to comment, "It's funky but not trendy, like a tavern should be, though I admit I have too goddamn many beer signs."

How to succeed in the tavern business is through hard work and liking people, Espe feels. "You have to be here. You have to stay and make a living at it, you can't hire everything out. You have to continually work on it."

Just like his marriage to Linda.

"People told me that if I went into the tavern business we'd be divorced in two years. Hell, we've been married 35 years and we're still really happy. Linda comes in and works at noon."

While he's doing quite well, Espe admits sadly that he thinks The

Hutch may be one of a vanishing breed.

"I don't know if neighborhood taverns are an endangered species; maybe they are. They seem to be anyway. You don't see them around like you used to, not like this one.

"But I will tell you thing," he says, grinning over at the mailmen who are making the old shuffleboard hum. "If I built a new one I'd design it just like this; an old-fashioned tavern for the average Joe."

Jake's Famous Crawfish Restaurant

401 S.W. 12th Ave.
503-226-1419

Joe G. Bianco

Skeptics who peer closely into Jake's lavish menu will discover that, yes, Oregon crawfish do indeed appear, lurking among other denizens plucked from Northwest waters to be served in one of the oldest and finest fish houses in the land.

For the uninitiated, the crawfish (crayfish to some) might be described as a dwarf lobster, a furtive, mini-clawed creature whose appearance on Jake's menu confirms that the restaurant has been serving "crawdads" (that's what we call them) since 1892.

A freshwater resident whose presence indicates the absence of pollution, crawdads once proliferated in the small streams, lakes and rivers in or near the cleaner, less crowded Portland of my youth.

Using nets or hands, we used to pull them up from the floor of Tryon and Fanno creeks, while the Tualatin River was once literally crawling with crawdads who, like the Columbia River salmon (alas, Jake's now serves the Alaska kind), have since been decimated by the exigencies of a rapacious population.

Today, though the Willamette River remains a convenient crawfishery, we are reminded that without the small crustaceans Jake's today might simply call itself a "Famous Old Portland Restaurant."

Which it is, a Portland historic landmark (the city's second oldest restaurant, after Huber's) that has been at its present site in the "Jake's Building" since the turn of the century.

The restaurant's namesake was Jacob Lewis Freiman, a colorful Portland character who built a reputation on the crawfish he served in the old Oregon Hotel.

That was in 1881, and by the time Jake had established his own restaurant, his skill at preparing seafood was known far and wide, drawing customers that included discriminating diners, travelers, visiting entertainers and others from Portland and across the land, including newspapermen, who embellished their stories in Jake's booths and bar.

"Jake's is one of the legends," says Larry Baldwin, a 41-year-old California 'legal alien,' and one of eight Jake's managers. "Wherever I go, visiting Jake's in Portland is one of the things many people have on their list of things to do."

A myth exists that Henry Weinhardt, when locating his new brewery in 1904, built just a block from Jake's so he might walk to his favorite restaurant—and sure enough, the venerable brick brewery with its landmark smokestack is still just a short stroll away.

Lingering in the restaurant today is a comfortable Gay '90s elegance that grabs you the moment you pass through the swinging doors of its popular corner bar. Above the bar is a sign counting down the days until St. Patrick's Day, while over a lavish display of bottled liquor, dominated by bottled ranks of single-malt Scotch and Irish whiskies, is a photograph of late President Richard Nixon, among other people to be found smiling down from among the memorabilia.

Jake's gleaming wood bar is a sturdy anachronism complete with a brass rail and a tiled trough recalling the days when men (mostly) stood, drank and chewed tobacco. The bar is served at various times by six bartenders, each natty in the same distinguishing white coats and dark bow ties that identify Jake's waiters.

Northwest beers are well represented at Jake's (remember the brewery across the street), and with a bow to its potted ferns, one feels quite at home in the bar, whether standing belly up or sitting at one of the small round tables with a view to the street.

Leaving the bar, the pervasive comfort of Jake's follows you through to its dark, labyrinthine dining rooms gleaming with polished wood, booths and tables crisp with white linen and sparkling with silver and glassware, the walls a gallery of paintings hanging on from the gilded age.

Most famous of these paintings is a Portland legend, the so-called "The Louvre Nude" ("Venus at the Bath," unsigned and undated, c. 1880), which hangs over the bar.

The painting was once owned by Thomas Kruse, founder of The Louvre Restaurant in the old Belvedere Hotel (Southwest Fourth Avenue and Alder Street), and in the Gay '90s' prolific nude-painting-above-the-bar-period "The Louvre Nude" was toasted often by last-century rakes as the most popular woman in town.

Other distinctive Northwest paintings, among some twenty in all purchased by various Jake's owners, are a view of Rooster Rock by the prolific pioneer primitive Eliza Barchus, famous for her haunting paintings of Mt. Hood (with or without a standing elk); a soon-to-be-completed Portland Hotel (demolished in 1952), painted in the 1880s by F. C. R. Grothjean; James Everett Stuart's depiction of Mt. Hood, and two paintings, "Willamette Falls at Oregon City" and "St. John's Bridge," done in the 1930s by H. L. Lopp.

In 1970, Jake's was added to a growing empire of restaurants managed by Portland entrepreneurs Bill McCormick and Doug Schmick, who, according to Baldwin, are currently linking Jake's name in a growing family of restaurants nationwide.

"We want to grow, yet maintain our legendary quality," explains Baldwin, a no-nonsense, managerial-looking guy who, like most Californians who come here, claims inevitably that he has fallen in love with Portland and with Jake's—which to any Portland native are synonymous.

As you might expect, Jake's lavish menu is described in superlatives emphasizing Northwest specialties of "quality, freshness and simplicity," with a veritable trawler's haul of seafood, for the most part, and anchored by the restaurant's "Famous Chocolate Truffle Cake."

In the bar, there is also an eclectic offering of happy hour finger food listed on a special menu for, at least on this day, what seem like ridiculously low prices.

Found evenings in the bar are assorted "suits," your stockbrokers, business folks and other spiffier types clawing their way to the top, as well as a sprinkling of young men and women languishing hopefully as they anticipate getting lucky in love.

And, often, handsful of tourists sprinkled in among artists, writers, newspaper folk, or the odd denizen from surrounding blocks, a neighborhood that might best be described as "interesting."

Much of Portland's gay night life rocks in the narrow streets nearby; Powell's City of Books, America's second largest bookstore, is down past the Blitz Brewery, as is a gathering of other bookstores, specialty shops, groceries, pizzerias, delis, taverns, apartments and hotels.

"The area is unique and lively," Baldwin observes, "but it's calmed down a lot too. Right now we're seeing a revival of the area, and business is great. We're busy night after night, and we don't have a slow day."

A new dining room was added to the back in 1977, but blended so smoothly into the Jake's Building it could have been there for a hundred years, the decorators having skillfully enhanced the restaurant's timeless character.

"Our philosophy has been very traditional," Baldwin explains, his words echoing from those towers of jargon where people create "P.R."

"Our bar, for example, we consider our 'tabernacle.' It's like a living room where you wait before going into dinner and, basically, is a reflection of everything we try to do..."

And Baldwin goes on like that for a while.

But I have lived in Portland all my life, and so has my father, I reflect, as Baldwin continues, young, eager and from San Diego. And in all that time I can never remember a time when Jake's had to try to do anything.

Now, as then, and not so long ago, when crawdads scudded their ragged claws across our once crystal-clear streams, Jake's is simply an Old Portland restaurant that continues serving up history, tradition...and very good food.

Jubitz Truck Stop

10210 N. Vancouver Way
503-283-1111

*"Old truck drivers just like
meat and potatoes...and they
throw gravy all over everything."*
Moe Jubitz

Some years ago during an interview with actress Shirley MacLaine, I was surprised to learn that she had driven alone to Portland from a home she has near Seattle.

During some small talk prior to the interview, Shirley mentioned driving down the I-5 freeway and pulling off for breakfast at a truck stop just this side of the Interstate Bridge.

"I had waffles," she said in her pixyish way, "and they were the best I've had in years. As soon as we're through here I'm going back for lunch."

And what place was that? I asked hungrily.

"The Jubitz Truck Stop," she replied. "Do you know it?"

Monroe "Moe" Jubitz stops midway across his truck stop's immense barroom floor, turns with a quizzical grin and says, "I wish I'd known that. Shirley MacLaine, you say...?"

We amble across the floor until Moe, who is 80, sits down at a table next to acres of dance floor. Above us, over the bandstand, a large banner reads "The Ponderosa," the sign bracketed at each end by large steely-eyed photographs of Clint and "The Duke" snarling down at the band—this night, appropriately, "Jeff and The Revolvers."

Obviously, we are in hard-core country-western country, and Moe, a gentle soul, says in a way that seems totally out of character, "I love country-western music. It's so much better than all that other junk you hear."

Moe's seemingly incongruous affection for things country, however, reminds us that in the pantheon of contemporary American heroes truck drivers and cowboys (who drive cows) share much of the same mythology.

In fact, as you see by their outfits—boots, jeans, plaid flannel shirts, wide leather belts and wider buckles—it is apparent that truckers who wanted to grow up to be cowboys fulfill this restless urge by crossing the prairies in Freightliners, Whites and Peterbilts.

After days on the trail, the vast interstate freeway system which Moe says makes truck driving "boring as hell," they arrive at truck stops like Jubitz' to feed, drink, rest and enjoy themselves.

With 30 acres and space for 300 trucks, with a motel, various restaurants, clothing stores, a laundry and three small theaters, the Jubitz Truck Stop is a modern Dodge City or Abilene, its spacious and friendly full-service bar the equivalent of the Long Branch Saloon.

"Miss Kitty" at Jubitz' Long Branch is Manager Jackie Murphy, an attractive 33-year-old woman with the long, lean, jeans-clad figure of a barrel racer, and loose red hair that sweeps the shoulders of her buckskin jacket.

Murphy has been working the truck stop bar for three and a half years, and if the look in Moe's eyes is what I think it is, a mixture of paternal pride and respect, she's been doing a damn good job.

Moe confirms this by saying, "I've had a lot of bar managers, but few really know the business like Jackie here."

Jackie confirms this by getting right to the point.

"We don't cater to the rowdies," she says in a firm Miss Kitty way, her words boring into my memory like six shots from a .44.

I envision suddenly the country-western bars of my past; places filled with "har-har!" louts, where fights were almost inevitable and, as the song says, "…The women all get prettier at closing time."

But not here.

"This is a wholesome bar," Murphy reiterates. "People say it's cozy and feels like home, and I'm going to keep it that way."

She looks me dead in the eye, and I have an urge to say, "Yes, Ma'am!"

And Moe interjects matter-of-factly, "We pay $65,000 a year in security to keep the drugs and undesirables out."

Having started the business in 1952, Moe added a restaurant and bar shortly after, acknowledging that "after being on the road all day truck drivers have to have some entertainment. Our restaurant and beer sales got us by for quite a while, and at one time we sold more beer per square foot than any tavern in Portland," he adds cryptically.

The huge and gleaming bar we see before us now, however, has been here in some form since 1968, remodeled after a fire a few years back. It's a comfortable, hunker-down kind of place with natural wood and soft lights, and Moe says, "You see those chrome truck bumpers on the wall? They look pretty classy, don't they?"

I admit they do, along with the red truck lights, the juke box and a large game room with three pool tables (down from eight a few years ago when, as Moe explains, "We used to be the biggest pool hall in town").

The lottery games are ranked along a wall near the bar, which is a large U-shaped counter that controls the room; on the side opposite the dance floor is a television the size of a 16-wheeler, in a lounge where truckers enjoy what Moe describes as "one of the finest lunches in town.

"There's a lot of meat!" Moe says, smacking his lips carnivorously. "It's good, all fresh. I eat here myself."

Murphy, who lives across the river in Vancouver, U.S.A., has been in the bar business for the past eight years. She emphasizes once again how she and her 17-person "crew" run a no-nonsense bar that offers truckers what they want.

"Oh sure, we've got hard liquor and a lot of different kinds of beer, including the fancy imported stuff. But when a guy sits down at the bar it's usually, 'gimme a Bud.'"

In addition to the drivers, the bar sees a lot of regulars, bar-hopping civilians with dancing feet from throughout the Portland-Vancouver area.

"This is a mellow crowd," Murphy explains once again. "They've 'been there, done that,' and just want to relax and have a good time. We make sure that they do."

Seeing that look in her eye once more, I recall the Marine Corps admonishment, "You *will* have fun!"

The Jubitz bar is open from 11 a.m. to 2 a.m., seven days a week, and featured along with its succulent luncheon buffet are live music and dancing each night.

The bar also offers line-dancing lessons, and Murphy says, "Line dancing is real big right now. Soon," she adds, looking carefully over at Moe, "we're going to need another dance floor."

Moe returns a look that says she can probably have anything she wants, then watches her proudly as she sashays away.

"...got to go," she says, her fingers flicking and tossing a wake of dark red hair.

Across the room, Moe's son Fred, who runs this part of the business, is in deep conversation with some salesmen; Al, Moe's other son, runs the company's transportation information division out in Beaverton.

Moe, on the other hand, certainly doesn't seem the kind of guy to have gotten into the truck stop business. A graduate of Portland's Lincoln High School, he studied liberal arts at Yale, where he was a southpaw pitcher on the school's Ivy League championship baseball team.

"I had chances to play with the Red Sox and Yankees farm teams," he says quietly, "but I didn't want to. And you know why? They were spitting tobacco all the time. That's right. I thought it was disgusting and wanted no part of it. I still love baseball, though," he adds quickly.

Moe got into the business on the ground floor, working for Bob Wilhelm years ago in Portland and learning all there was to know, from bookkeeping to truck mechanics.

"I never drove, though," he confesses, looking off wistfully. "That's too tough on your body—and on marriages."

Then he surprises you by leaning over and pushing his nose to one side, blurting, "You see this broken nose? One of Dave Beck's boys gave it to me."

Now a gentle, soft-spoken white-haired man, in his lifetime Moe has climbed Mt. Hood 40 times and, slowing down now, misses the energy of his youth—the years when he was building the truck stop up from nothing and loving every minute of it.

I feel this love later, when before I leave he insists on showing me around. We leave the bar and walk through the kitchen into the 24-hour restaurant—and everyone calls out, "Hi, Moe!"

Then we cross the truck lot, pass the tire shop, enter the snack shop— and along the way everyone says, "Hi, Moe!"

After we climb the stairs to "The Top of the Stop" and enter Moe's pride and joy, the "307 Club," named after the nearby freeway exit, a plush lounge, beer bar and computer center for drivers, there are more "Hi, Moe!"'s offered with obvious warmth for a man respected as founder and patriarch of this tiny, beneficient kingdom.

Later, as we walk back to the bar, he says, "Truckers are a different kind of people, and you hear a lot of things about drivers that just aren't true. They work hard and it's a difficult job, especially being on the freeway all day, and they're away from home a lot. There are a lot of broken marriages."

Back inside, there are a few more polite "Hi, Moe!"'s he acknowledges with a casual wave, and after sitting down he continues, "You know, truck drivers are pretty particular. You know what they want in a place like this? I'll tell you: It isn't the booze, because they don't drink like they used to. No, it's good food. And you know what's next? Cleanliness. How about that?"

Then Moe leans back, smiling almost smugly, and I know he's enjoyed the day and telling his stories.

He's proud of this place and what he's done, and says, "You know why we're so popular? We've got everything a trucker wants right here. At the end of a long day they can come in and have a good time."

But then he adds, "Shirley MacLaine! Damn! I wish I'd been here."

Kelly's Olympian

426 S.W. Washington St.
503-228-3669

Back in my mean old drinking days, when I walked the downtown streets missing buses that could take me where my family wanted me to be, Kelly's Olympian was a place I avoided like the plague.

Trapped in folly and not yet realizing that, in my case at least, "drink takes the man," I looked upon Kelly's as a final surrender; not quite skid road, yet the entranceway to a netherworld where, I conceived in my hazy imagination, all hope might be abandoned if one entered there.

In those days, certainly, a view through Kelly's swinging doors offered visions of the abyss: desperate men drinking day and night beneath harsh fluorescent lights, playing cards, their minds clouded by booze and tobacco smoke; a non-nonsense drinkers' bar where these same desperate men faced eternity with vacant, thousand-yard stares.

Late in my drinking career, which ended some time ago, I did find myself in Kelly's. It was an evening of late-summer languor with a hint of fall in the air, a night when I missed too many buses and Kelly's neon sign seduced me like a devil in green.

"So what did you think?" asks Greg Powers, the current owner, as we sit over coffee in Kelly's Olympic-sized restaurant and saloon.

When I say I can't remember, being what it was then, he pulls at his short graying beard, smiles warmly and explains, "Kelly's isn't that way anymore."

At 52, Greg is an affable Portlander who attended Grant and Lincoln high schools, served in the Marine Corps during the Vietnam War, and, after a hitch at Portland State University, came into the business that has involved the Powers family since 1928.

"Actually it was 1929," interjects Greg's father Keith, who eases into the booth with his second, much younger wife Lucia, the old man's companion since 1959.

"I was the mean old lady who made them get rid of the cuspidors," Lucia says as a way of introduction. "If they were going to chew tobacco, I made them go outside."

After giving his wife a loving glance, Keith, a garrulous old gentleman of 82, begins stories that began long before his own father, E. Gilbert Powers, started at Kelly's nearly 70 years before.

As Keith spins his yarns, I learn that Kelly's long history began during Portland's gilded age, in the years before the turn of the century when John Kelly and a group of partners opened the original saloon a few blocks away (it has been at its present location since 1957).

Keith explains that Kelly's surname, "Olympian," has little to do with athletics, but was suggested "by an old fellow named Brown who was an accountant for the Olympia Brewery in Tumwater, Wash. The brewery put up money to help Kelly get started back in 1902."

Kelly's still serves Olympia Beer, by the way, along with some 47 domestic and foreign brews, including a large representation from the Northwest's fine and growing microbreweries.

(Greg suggests that serious beer drinkers curious about Kelly's multifarious labels join the saloon's "Beer Club and Hall of Foam" and sample them all).

In its halcyon days under John Kelly's capable and exacting hand, Kelly's earned a reputation as one of the finest eating and drinking establishments on the West Coast—no mean feat in a once rip-roaring seaport whose often notorious saloons, exemplified by the legendary Erickson's, were known around the world.

Like so many saloons in the old days, Kelly's was known as a "men's resort," a place where workingmen could relax, play cards, smoke and chew to their hearts' content, while enjoying reasonably priced square meals and generous drinks, without the distraction of women.

Until fairly recently, in fact, there was no women's rest room in Kelly's, and signs proclaimed not so subtly that "ladies" were less than welcome.

That has all changed, of course, with women now more than welcome in Kelly's, though still accepted grudgingly by a hardcore of oldtime male denizens who are slowly fading away.

"The backbone of our business used to be single working guys who lived in hotels and rooming houses downtown," Greg explains. "But now most of these are gone, and many of my old customers are dead."

His father remembers farther back, when downtown Portland was a much different place. With a youthful gleam in his eye, he begins a litany of saloons, bars and cardrooms that glow in his memory like gaslights.

"Hell, there were cardrooms all over town! Erickson's, the Clover Club, Alaska Cardroom and Lunch, the Caribou, Stockman's, Dahl & Penne's…people used to play cards. They didn't have cars or televisions, and a lot more people lived downtown. Loggers would come in from the woods for the winter and hole up in cheap, clean residential hotels. There were always people on the streets and you weren't afraid to come downtown. It was a lot safer in the old days," he adds with a cheerful melancholy.

"Let me give you an example," he continues, warming to the subject, while Greg and Lucia sit grinning at the old man's yarns.

"Right up the street there used to be a nice little bar in the old Perkins Hotel. You remember? Rich's Cigar Store was nearby and there was that big bronze bull in an alcove up on the roof...?

"Well," Keith continues, "I liked the place because there were always a lot of nicely dressed men and women in the bar. They were soft-spoken and real polite, and there was never any trouble. You could relax in a place like that.

"Anyway, I used to pop in from time to time, when it was quiet here, and one day I was sitting there about four o'clock, enjoying the company of these well-behaved, elegant customers, when the bartender suddenly starts shouting, 'All right! All you whores and pimps get out of here!' The bar emptied like a fire drill and I was the only guy left in the place."

Keith grins again, letting his eyes move to a table where two nicely dressed young women are "doing lunch."

"Portland was like that then," he says. "Sometimes you didn't know whether you were in a sea story or a fairy tale."

Looking around, I see what he means. Though having been spared the precious fern-bar metamorphosis of so many older drinking places, Kelly's has succeeded in rounding off its rough edges while retaining its distinctive, semi-tough atmosphere. A long stand-up bar still dominates the left side of the cavernous, high-ceilinged drinking hall, but gone are the headachy fluorescent lights that were capable of blasting hangovers into nuclear nightmares.

Under much softer lights are booths and tables for eating, drinking and passing the time. And where you once encountered a cast of characters suitable for a play by Eugene O'Neill, you are more apt to find a respectable clientele of men and women who know what it means to "do lunch."

"From what used to be primarily a workingman's bar," Greg explains, "we now see a lot of downtown office workers, business and professional people, as well as a younger crowd, especially at night when we have live music.

"And St. Patrick's Day, of course. You can't forget that. It's our busiest day of the year."

Meals at Kelly's include not only lunch and dinner, but a "good breakfast too," he adds, reminding that Kelly's opens at 6:30 a.m. (closing time is midnight on weekdays and 2 a.m. on weekends) and that many of his breakfast customers are commuters headed for offices downtown.

After decades of meals that once simply stuck chow onto the ribs of men who lifted, loaded, and logged all day, Kelly's now offers a more varied menu planned by a capable chef: seafood, sandwiches, steak, chicken and the usual suspects, along with daily specials—and breakfast throughout the day.

Every night but Sunday and Monday the music comes in, live offerings of blues, jazz and rock-and-roll, as well as oldtime popular favorites, and a singer from time to time.

Take a poll of the Powers family; they all love the place and wouldn't trade it for the world. Greg, with a wife and young children in the suburbs, is a romantic who loves Kelly's history and tradition, but his customers most of all.

He began with his father after leaving the Corps, "and now I think of it as an oldtime Southwest Portland social club. Do I like it? I must; I'm here every day."

Keith started with his father back in 1938, then bought into the business after World War II.

He laughs and shakes his head. "I was going to stay in the Air Force. You know, make it a career. But my dad said, 'Buy in or I'm going to sell the goddamn place.' I don't regret it a bit."

Lotus Cardroom & Café

932 S.W. 3rd Ave.
503-227-6185

Back in the good old bad days of the Lotus Cardroom & Café, if you had to go in there, it was best to move low, slow and inconspicuously so you didn't stir anyone's wrath and perhaps draw gunfire.

A professional gambler and boozer (and God knows what else?) I knew, from my own bad old drinking days, an habitué of the Lotus who complained of having to have his suits altered to accommodate his shoulder holster, told me of the night he pulled his Roscoe on an unfortunate companion during an altercation at the bar.

"Before I could think, I had my gun to his head and was about to blow him away," the gambler, who has since reformed, recalled, then added, "That was the night I quit drinking."

Less fortunate was the Lotus bartender gunned down by a dishwasher back in the down-and-dirty days, a time not so long ago when the Lotus was unofficial headquarters to a demi-monde of hookers, pimps and drug dealers who conducted business on the corner outside.

"When I was a kid," says Jeff Plew, 37, the current manager and a native Portlander, "I was afraid to walk down the street around here."

"Yeah, and they'd all come in here and drink," says bartender Anna Karns, a tough, 17-year-veteran of the Lotus who recalls the "good old days" with the enthusiasm with which an old Marine might recall combat on Guadacanal.

"It's a lot better now," Karns adds, looking up from a bucket of ice she is pouring beneath the bar: a great, obviously hard-worn cherrywood antique that is fourteen feet high, thirty feet long and, like so many old Western bars, had seen hard service on the frontier—first in Tombstone, Arizona, and later, up north in an Aberdeen, Washington, whorehouse before finding a home in the Lotus decades ago.

It is rumored around town that its twin was once a fixture in Portland's legendary but now vanished Hoyt Hotel, whose "Gay '90s Bar" was once a popular and fashionable watering hole.

On the back bar a sign reads "261 days until Fat Tuesday"—Fat Tuesday being, of course, the last day of annual revels during New Orleans' famed Mardi Gras, and for the past six years, under the management of Concept Entertainment Group, Inc., celebrated in the Lotus as well.

"It's become a tradition," Plew explains, looking over his shoulder to a wall opposite the bar, where there is a gallery of mounted animal heads whose centerpiece is a huge moose flanked by other unfortunate creatures that include a stoic mountain sheep, a wild boar, a pronghorned antelope; over there a gazelle, as well as a large stuffed fish which I thought was a marlin, but which turned out to be a sailfish instead.

After commenting on the beheaded menangerie, Plew grins and says the atmosphere hasn't changed that much since the old days—which it hasn't. Looking around, one can see wood seasoned by decades of smoke and despair segueing into dim walls surrounding booths plump with genuine vinyl.

But the crowd has. In the early days there was a hotel upstairs (an old sign still reads: "Furnished Rooms 3rd Floor—Ring Elevator Bell"), and the Lotus was transient home to loggers, longshoremen, railroad workers and others who in the past swirled "dime-a-dance" girls through oceans of whiskey and fogs of cigar smoke.

Once, before the neighborhood's cheap and once prolific hotels and boarding houses went down like ripe wheat before urban redevelopment, pensioners gathered in the Lotus to drink, reminisce and play cards at tables in the back.

Turning again to a blank wall near the kitchen, Plew explains, "Until recently, there used to be a huge call board there listing jobs available for men who drifted in looking for work."

The Lotus' Old Portland atmosphere has also attracted filmmakers. Gus Van Zant used the hotel upstairs in his movie "My Own Favorite Idaho," and Plew points to a booth that was used in a commercial for the Oregon Lottery Commission (video poker machines are up next to the bar).

"There is also a ghost," Plew confesses delightedly. "Weird things go on in the basement, and I think it may be the ghost of someone who was murdered there a long time ago. At least that's what I've heard. I know that when I go down there funny things happen with the lights."

"Yeah," Chef Jeffery McChesney adds enthusiastically, "and there may be another, the ghost of a kid who overdosed on drugs some years ago."

McChesney, 26, is a native of Gladstone and a graduate of Portland's Western Culinary Institute—"When Horst Mager still had it," he assures me—who cooked for some years in New York City before recently returning home.

The chef runs over to the kitchen and returns with a menu that is eclectic and wholesome, but which, along with the predictable offerings of trendier restaurants these days, is seasoned with items redolent of the Old South and compatible with the Lotus' rather incongruous tribute to Fat Tuesday.

"I guess you could describe our food as kind of like what mom used to cook, if she could cook," McChesney says with a twinkle in his eye. "Or you could call it 'eclectic American home style' with a Southern flair."

Whatever. Though Plew promises that the Lotus' famous old fried chicken stand outside on the corner will be replaced by a pasta bar and a "much healthier menu of takeout cuisine."

Which is good news for the yuppies, and for those who will soon inhabit the huge new federal office building being completed across the street.

While still free of the ferns and other slick and precious bibelots that make so many new places seem the same, the Lotus' clientele is a mixed bag of young, old, women and men, with a lingering vestige of much older denizens Karns remembers from the past.

There is a full bar, eight draft beers, a good representation of Northwest brews, and a wide selection of bottled beers that should please almost anyone.

Above, the Lotus has ceilings that seem to rise up forever, and a browse through on a quiet rainy Portland afternoon requires a romantic imagination and a fondness for things nostalgic.

Outside, if you zip down to Second Avenue and look toward the back of the Lotus, you will see painted on the old brick a huge mural, swirling with color and depicting how the Lotus used to be.

On weekends, however, even the ghost runs for cover as the quiet weekday Lotus is transformed into a nightclub, with the dancing feet of a new generation of denizens moving to D.J.-picked tunes blasting through "Theme Nights," Wednesday through Sunday.

As it was explained to me once by a young woman, "Here you have your '70s, your '80s retro, your current...and like that."

Yes, well...?

But it's "great," according to Plew, who before this job operated the "In-Between" tavern at Welches, on the way to Mt. Hood.

"I enjoy my customers as well as the people who work in the industry," he says eagerly.

"And I can gab all day," Plew adds, laughing. "It's a perfect business for me to be in."

Lotus hours are 11 a.m. to 2 a.m. Monday-Friday; 8 a.m. to 2 a.m. Saturday and Sunday—and since lunch is crowded, plan ahead.

Reflecting back through all the years I have known the Lotus, and from stories of those who have known the place longer than I, I ask Karns, the old veteran, if things are really that much better now.

A sturdy, redheaded woman with the unsmiling demeanor of a Marine Corps gunnery sergeant, Karns rattles down another bucket of ice before answering. It requires some thought, for she has worked at Erickson's, the Caribou Club and some other tough, legendary but now defunct skid road bars where life could often be as cheap as the whiskey.

When she looks up finally, the ice snugged down, she says bluntly, "Better? You're damn right it's better! These are good people to work for."

It's a nice thing to consider when leaving through the Lotus' battered old swinging doors.

Nick's Famous Coney Island

3746 S.E. Hawthorne Blvd.
503-235-4024

Joe G. Bianco

To cross the mosaic threshold of Nick's Famous Coney Island is to enter a time warp where it will always be the late 1940s or early 1950s, when America seemed a safer, saner place to be.

While outside Portland's Hawthorne Boulevard is becoming yet another upscale strip pandering to the terminally trendy, inside the ambiance is that of a battered baseball glove: comfortable, worn and unpretentiously human.

"People say it reminds them of an old New York place," says owner Frank Nudo, 63, who took over from original owner Nick Carlascio back in 1960. Carlascio had run a regular restaurant, with breakfasts and everything, since 1934. But in recent years it's been Coneys, mostly, as well as hamburgers, cheeseburgers, tuna fish (for the health freaks) and Nick's famous macaroni salad.

"Nick taught me how to make the salad," Nudo says proudly. "You come in, have a sandwich, some salad, and it's a good lunch," he adds in a street-smart, big-city dialect of someone you might think was nurtured east of the Mississippi—or at least Chicago. Not surprisingly, the Chicago Cubs are his favorite baseball team—"I live and die with the Cubs," he announces proudly. He admits to being a sports fanatic who remembers the golden days when Nick's was a popular hangout for local sports reporters. A few still drop by now and then, the ones who have survived life's bad weather and what newspapers have become.

Nudo remembers when Nick's was a prime mover in Portland's intramural tavern sports leagues. "I used to sponsor everything: Little League, bowling, softball—you name it. I got trophies in the back you wouldn't believe," announces the short, stocky, dark-haired man with the bull voice of an umpire calling balls and strikes.

Paradoxically, Nudo is really from the tiny farm community of Stanfield, in Eastern Oregon, and has lived in Portland since 1944. A graduate of

Cleveland High, he worked for Nick two years before taking over the restaurant, which happens to be in his old neighborhood. "We used to hang around Nick's when we were kids," he shouts warmly. "I never been more than five blocks from home."

Nudo jumps to his feet now and then, announcing abruptly, "I got to stir the pot…!" The pot is filled with Coney Island sauce, a chili mix concocted spicier than average by Nudo, who likes it hot. When this dangerously delicious ambrosia is poured over one or two long hot dogs in an open bun, with or without onions, and served in a paper-lined basket, you've got a "Coney"—and the best in town.

Coneys are 70 percent of what Nudo sells, along with some beer—"People don't sit around here and drink," he barks—in what is essentially a sports bar. The walls, shelves and back bar are a museum of artifacts from baseball, basketball, boxing, hockey and other sports, with photographs and fading newspaper clippings climbing the dark walls above the comfortable booths. Behind the bar is a clutter of treasures: an autographed photo of Bob Feller, legendary ace Cleveland Indians' pitcher of the 1940s; a signed photo of country-western singer Dolly Parton; the signature the late heavyweight boxing champion Rocky Marciano left long ago; and autographed baseballs. scattered about like an infield after batting practice. There is even an authentic New York Yankee jersey splayed up on one wall like a bear hide.

Back from stirring the pot, Nudo brings over a shrink-wrapped baseball signed by Carl Erskine, a newly acquired treasure for his trove. "Look at this!" he says, rolling his eyes and waving his arms like a man calling for a fly ball. "Someone just sent it to me. People bring in all kinds of stuff. I don't collect the stuff, it just comes in. Look at it!" he says again, arms in the air.

Nudo works his Coneys with three employees: Kenny Kell, an enigmatic, stern-faced gentleman known for some reason as "The Commander," who has been with Nudo 30 years; and Herb Chin and Mike Lauro, each with 20 years service at Nick's.

Nudo leaves again to stir the pot, and when he returns this time he is more serious. He talks about the street and neighborhood, how thing aren't the way they used to be, lamenting the rise of crime, people's lack of respect for one another—values that somehow got lost between the year Nick's opened and now, but which have been retained by his longtime customers. "Listen, the only way I've survived 35 years in this business is because of my regulars," Nudo says firmly. "They're good people, my customers.

"And sure, business has tailed off, people eating healthier and all. But," he adds with a broad grin, "every now and then they just let themselves go and have a Coney." Then he's up again, on his feet and heading for the kitchen, and without looking back I can hear him say, "Got to stir the pot!"

Nob Hill Bar & Grill

937 N.W. 23rd Ave.
503-274-9616

Mike Ryerson sits quietly at the bar drinking coffee, smoking and shaking his head over the morning paper, recalling the time when he owned the Nob Hill Bar & Grill, then called Nobby's, and the longshoreman was playing pool and fell through the floor.

"The pool table was right over there," Ryerson, a local newspaperman, explains, turning slowly and pointing to where the tiny kitchen is now.

"He was setting up a shot when the floor collapsed and he went right on through to the basement."

Ryerson admits the place needed a lot of work when he owned it, back when the tavern's hollower-eyed denizens represented the neighborhood's hardcore drinking class; back before Mother Goose touched her wand to Northwest 23rd Avenue and transformed a funky everyman's district into a playground and boutique for the terminally hip.

But not anymore. Nobby's, its floor repaired and strengthened, has been upscaled to the Nob Hill Bar & Grill. And while the odd denizen may still reappear to swill suds and scowl at the Eddie Bauer paradigms wandering past outside, a light-handed gentrification has attracted customers with a drier, softer core.

Surprisingly, this rebirth has been accomplished while retaining the residual funky charm of the place, which current owners Greg and Barbara Hermans maintain as on oldtime Northwest Portland tavern.

In fact, if you talk to other oldtimers like Ryerson, who, like me, has lived in Portland all of his life, this the last of a vanishing breed in Northwest Portland, the others having disappeared or been overwhelmed by chic makeovers.

"People say we're crazy for not cashing in on the gentrification going on around us. And I supposed we could be making a lot more money if we fixed it up more," says Barbara, a cheerful, chatty woman of 35 with two small children at home, "but we wanted to keep it the same, and we will as long as we can."

"If it works don't fix it," Greg, a serious, less talkative man of 36, interjects succinctly as he moves back and forth from the kitchen.

A former sales rep, he bought the Nob Hill from his father Larry in 1989, does all the cooking, and when he disappears again Barbara explains how they met in the tavern nine years ago. They live nearby at Northwest 23rd and Hoyt.

Beyond its small bar and kitchen, where Greg is flipping eggs over-easy and snuggling them next to hash browns for the morning crowd, the Nob Hill is a large wood-paneled expanse surrounding a gathering of tables where people are eating, drinking coffee or just passing the time.

There are three television sets for sporting events, a pool table, and lottery games are sequestered inobtrusively in a small alcove behind swinging door.

Memories of the rich old neighborhood are preserved in a collection of photographs: the street as it was, a trolley car in the snow near the tavern, and the tavern itself in one of its earlier incarnations.

According to Barbara, who has tracked the tavern back through time, it began in 1929 as a restaurant owned by one Mrs. Laura May. Vacant in 1930, it was revived as a restaurant the next year when it was owned by a "Loren C.," then by J. B. Bucholz; from 1935 to 1944 it was the Adams Sisters' Café.

From 1949 to 1957 it was the Dunsmoor Inn, then the Nobby Tavern we already know.

Prominent on the Nob Hill's menu is a photograph that recalls Portland's once glorious baseball past: a picture of the Nob Hill Baseball Team of 1893 framed around its manager, Dan Malarkey.

Those old enough will recall the city's fine old Vaughn Street Ballpark, as well as the clanging, open-sided trolleys—the "Ballpark Specials"—that delivered fans to the games (double-headers on Sunday) where they could watch the Portland Beavers battle it out with teams in the once highly acclaimed Pacific Coast League.

Baseball fans still gravitate to the Nob Hill, where in recent seasons the Hermans have provided buses to the Portland Rockies games, now played in Civic Stadium—which is carpeted and not quite the same, but baseball nevertheless.

The tavern also sponsors a slow-pitch softball team and two basket-ball teams; there are some who bowl, and when you ask him, Greg will admit, "Yeah, I guess you could call it a sports bar, though I still like to think of it as a neighborhood tavern."

Once a posh neighborhood of elegant homes owned by Portland's carriage trade, Northwest Portland ("Nob Hill" refers to "nob," an archaic reference to a person of wealth or social standing), according to demographers, now represents the highest urban residential density on the West Coast.

Contained with the district is a vibrant mix of residents that includes artists, writers and musicians, the affluent as well as upwardly mobile members of the middle class, while still retaining a tough and tattered population of working people, drifters young and old, and a sizable number of pensioners inhabiting its myriad living spaces.

Cater-corner from the Nob Hill is the vast Good Samaritan Hospital, known to everyone in Portland as "Good Sam," and hospital employees are among the tavern's most frequent and loyal patrons.

"But for some reason we get very few tourists," Greg comments, referring to the hordes who stomp the avenue and prowl its shops and restaurants on evenings and weekends.

"They seem to hit the other restaurants along Twenty-third," Barbara adds, "but they tend to avoid us, and I don't know why. We're on the busiest corner, 23rd and Lovejoy, but for some reason they pass us by."

Then smiling as if she doesn't care (which she doesn't,; business is still good), Barbara comments playfully, "Maybe they don't think we're hip enough."

If so, they're missing out on a pleasant Northwest experience. Like most Portland taverns these days, as much food is being sold as booze—probably more, because people don't drink like they used to. The Nob Hill admits minors until 3 p.m.; regular hours are from 8 a.m. to 2:30 a.m.

In addition to breakfast and a brunch on weekends, the tavern has a full menu that includes "Good Sam Burgers," "Good Sam-wiches," "Good Sam-baskets" (fish and chips, chicken, finger steak), soups and salads, and a list of side orders, soft drinks and other beverages.

But no dinners or pizza, Greg claiming that pizza "kind of competes with the burgers," which are a Nob Hill specialty.

Found at the bar is a full offering of libations foreign and domestic, including the products of several mostly Portland microbreweries.

Barbara attributes the Hermans' success and satisfaction with the Nob Hill to its staff—"They don't put up with any nonsense," she says—and to the tavern's loyal and friendly customers.

"Around here," she says, "most of our old customers don't have to worry about drinking and driving home. Most of them walk here from their homes, and many have known each other for years."

She laughs again, a transplant from Ohio who now would never think of living anywhere else but Portland.

"I met Greg in Nobby's; a lot of people meet each other here, and I've seen people propose to each other in the tavern. It's that kind of place."

Greg returns from the grill where breakfast is beginning to segue into lunch, sizzling burgers crowding the sausage links, bacon and ham.

Then I ask them both, "What makes a good tavern?"

While Greg looks down at the floor and thinks for a moment, Barbara grabs his arm and gives him a hug.

"You're looking at him," she says lovingly.

Greg grins at her, then without a word slips back to the grill.

Pal's Shanty

4630 N.E. Sandy Blvd.
503-288-9732

In this town, whenever someone mentions crab cocktails, someone will mention Pal's Shanty, Portland's venerable Hollywood District tavern, whose success has been achieved through the reputation of those succulent marine crustaceans.

"When I first started crab cocktails back in 1967," says Marty Hanson, who has owned the tavern longer than that, "cocktails were fifty cents. Now they're eight dollars, but they still sell like crazy."

"That's right," adds Jim Hanson, her son and business partner. "At one time we were going through two thousand pounds a week."

I start to add this up, and figure no matter how large the servings (a family secret) that's enough cocktails, crab cakes, crêpes, salad, "Hangtown Fry" and related sandwiches to deplete a small-sized Oregon bay.

But maybe I heard Jim wrong? Maybe he was referring to all the seafood sold at Pal's: Dungenesss crab, clams (steamer or razor), halibut and calamari (squid to you), a sea harvest so bountiful that we might easily forget the Shanty's original intent was selling beer.

Or maybe he was thinking about the days when his father, Marty's late husband Cliff, was in charge of the kitchen—a former Air Force mess sergeant trained in preparing vast meals for squadrons of men: "Crack three hundred crabs, add forty quarts of cocktail sauce, slice seven dozen lemons…"

That sort of thing.

Marty sits next to me and digs into a platter of golden fried razor clams, my personal seafood favorite, and my mouth begins to water.

"My husband loved to cook," she says, looking off to a place where Cliff might be making "S.O.S." beyond the wild blue yonder.

Marty explains how she and Cliff got the crab cocktail idea during a long-ago visit to San Francisco's Fishermen's Wharf, sometime back in the 1960s, when things seafood-wise were different everywhere.

"'We could serve 'em with beer,' Cliff told me…and so we left California…"

"You mean…?"

Marty looks at Jim, who looks at his sister Sharon back in the kitchen, who looks warily at Mom, who has stopped eating her razor clams.

"That's right, we're Californians," Marty says defiantly, though adding quickly, "But we've been here since 1965."

"Moved here to get away from L.A.," Jim adds almost apologetically.

Which I assume means that they've been naturalized, and therefore everything is okay.

At 76, Marty is a tough but friendly woman who says she won't retire because she loves the business and her customers too much.

"I'm still the boss," she says firmly, a fact obviously not in dispute by the expressions on the faces of her son and daughter.

Jim, 47, is a Vietnam veteran on 80-percent disability, and Sharon once owned a Westside adjunct of Pal's that is no more.

"I did it for three years but became exhausted," Sharon explains, while Marty makes it plain that the former "Pal's Shanty West" is now simply "The Shanty," and under new owners.

"Don't get them confused," she warns, pointing a fork redolent with clam and tartar sauce.

How Pal's got started, no one knows for sure—"There's all kinds of stories," Marty says.

It was Pal's Shanty before the Hansons, and Marty has traced the building back to the 1920s, when it was a small silent movie theatre known as the "Elite."

"The lobby was over there," she says, scowling and pointing her fork to a gaggle of blinking, tinkling lottery games (which she doesn't like).

"We used to have a pool table, and before that shuffleboard," Jim interjects. "But people want the machines now. It's like we've got to have them to be competitive."

Unchanged and customer-friendly, Pal's Shanty is an old neighborhood tavern evolved into a popular eating place without the upscale transformations of many other such places.

Beer is still drawn from taps affixed to a unique little log cabin structure behind the bar (which may have given Pal's its name); the bar has stools, and the tables are another story.

"Did you see my agate tables?" Marty asks, pointing proudly to large heavy discs of highly polished stones. "I had those made by a blind man in Gold Beach."

The tables are beautiful and shiny, their tops reflecting Pal's brightly lighted menu hanging behind the bar. Beneath an admonition to drink the "Un-Cola" are listed not only Pal's seafood specialties, but sandwiches, burgers ("the best in town," of course), salads, soup, chowder (a Portland radio station gave Pal's its Best Clam Chowder award two years in a row)—"and we make our own chili," Marty points out.

"We do a lot of things the hard way," Marty says, sated by a tummy filled with clams. "For example, we slice our own roasts and make our own thousand islands dressing."

Pal's fish and seafood, increasingly hard to come by, sadly, in a time of pollution and diminishing resources, are always top quality and supplied by "reliable sources up north."

"We are the best seafood restaurant in Oregon," Ruth, a waitress at Pal's for twenty-five years, interjects flatly.

Pal's also has a reliable reputation for always being packed.

Lunches are big with the local business people, while dinners are popular with everyone, especially families, and are served until 10:30 p.m.—"We get hungry crowds of all ages and sizes," Marty says.

"Food used to be only a sideline," she adds, "but now we get people from all over the country. We just had a crowd in from New Orleans, which is flattering considering the number of legendary seafood restaurants there."

Not just the food, but the atmosphere attracts Pal's customers, who consider it a kind of pub, though the ambiance is unmistakably 1950s funky. Old neighborhood denizens still drop by, but Marty says these are disappearing.

"Those who are still alive come in," she says, "but now it seems like there's a funeral every week."

Then she leaks a rare laugh that reveals a crack in her tough demeanor.

"People know their tables, and when they come in that's what they want. During lunch one time we had two guys, well-dressed business-men, get into a fight over a table by the window."

Not to forget, beer, wine and a good selection of local microbrews are available, though Pal's hard-drinking days are over. Now it's a good place to eat in a good part of old Portland known as Hollywood.

Before leaving, I decide to try once more: "So, Marty," I ask, "just how much crab is in those cocktails anyway?"

"I told you," she says playfully, "it's a family secret. Let's just say the customers are always happy."

The Portsmouth Club & Lounge

5264 N. Lombard St.
503-285-8863

To live and die in North Portland means having had at least one close encounter with The Portsmouth Club and Lounge, a legendary landmark for those living and working in the city's far corner.

In previous incarnations The Portsmouth Club was a dark rumor on the edge of Portland's widely scattered tavern demi-monde, a place where life, even if you didn't want it to, might grab you and pull you in. Those who listened to the rumors were hard drinkers like myself, denizens of downtown or southwest Portland, who in our cups preferred to avoid places divided by reputation into a "dirty side" and a "good side," which was the way the Portsmouth Club used to be before Chris Penner, a young entrepreneur in his 30s, took over several years ago. (Penner's dad Doug owns the Twilight Room just across the street, a popular college hangout where Chris began his apprenticeship as a fry cook at the tender age of thirteen.)

Where once customers mingled with an element described, with great understatement, as shady, "now," Penner explains, "it's a nice, quiet place. We've lost the troublesome customers and got the ones we wanted." Chris' mother Janet (Doug's wife), her son's partner, elaborates, "There was a lot of drug stuff going on when we took over, but that's been run out," she explains pleasantly, "and some of our former customers are in prison now."

Having had seven owners and as many different names since it began as a saloon back in 1917, the club has always been The Portsmouth Club to neighborhood habitués. "No one ever called it anything else," Janet says. Today, the former "clean side" remains "The Portsmouth Club Lounge," while the old "dirty side" has been transformed into "Mama Gianetta's," a clean, well-lighted appendage whose menu proclaims: "Great Italian Food, Famous since 1993."

Entering on the lounge side, "cleaner and brighter than ever before," Chris boasts expansively, customers are greeted by a large tank of tropical fish whose lazily circling presence seems almost a symbol guaranteeing the Portsmouth's peace and tranquility. One must assume that these exotic and colorful creatures would not reside in a place where an errant pool cue or playfully tossed beer bottle might invade their home and send them gasping and flopping to the floor.

There are three pool tables, dart boards, a large television and a clutch of lottery games, as well as a full-service bar enhanced by recent renovations whose dark wood paneling, carpets and comfortable booths have transformed the Portsmouth into a cozier, more pub-like atmosphere where conversation has replaced cultural conflict. "We used to have live music and dancing," Chris says, pointing to a large juke box, "but that caused a lot of trouble. We've got a good crowd now, and no one seems to mind."

In the old days The Portsmouth was a hangout for longshoremen and shipyard workers from Port facilities on Swan Island and the Willamette, many of whom would drop by for "eye-openers" when the club opened at 7 a.m. Today, while tough old North Portland continues to be tenderized by gentrification, anachronisms can still be seen entering through The Portsmouth's doors. Arriving each day for the 4 p.m. cocktail hour are older folks who walk to the Club from homes in a still-tightly-knit neighborhood.

Lunch, on the other hand, sees a lot of the district business people, while the evening and weekend crowd is a mixed bag—though everyone, young and old, mingles congenially to provide a balance that keeps the lid on.

Mama Gianetta's (11 a.m. to 9 p.m.), under the control of chef Roberta Bond, features an extensive and elaborate Italian menu (children under 10 eat free with an adult dinner), and both Janet and Chris, understandably—for this was once the club's dirty side—consider Mama Gianetta's "the nicest restaurant in North Portland."

Back from fiddling with a temperamental cigarette machine, Chris gets right to the point: "Today we're open 9 to 2 a.m. seven days a week…" while Janet adds, "…except Christmas, Easter and Thanksgiving." A tall young man in glasses who appears less like a barkeep than a cost accountant, Chris studied hotel-restaurant management at Portland Community College but leaves the accounting up to Janet, a willowy woman who quickly reminds you this is a family business, a labor of love. Settling down next to her son, her husband prospering across the street, Janet conveys the confidence the Penner family enjoys from running a tight ship.

"The family has the corner, well…cornered," Janet admits good-naturedly. "But it wasn't by design. When the Club became available, we simply said, 'Let's do it!' We've lived here a long time, and since our lives are invested in the neighborhood it seemed the thing to do."

Like Chris, she loves not only the business but the people they serve.

"Sure," Chris says simply, "I always wanted to be my own boss. Remember, I grew up in the business. And whenever I want, I can pop over and talk to dad about what's going on."

Janet laughs. "It seems to be working," she says to Chris, "he's starting to take your advice."

History by the Glass

Produce Row Café

204 S.E. Oak St.
503-232-8355

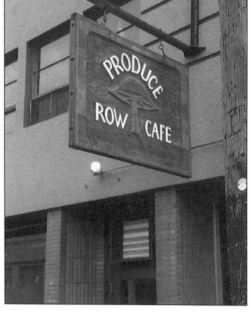

Mid-morning on a gray Portland day, and the produce district has a quiet feel of anticipation, like any minute a big old freight train will roll in and drop off a lot of fruit and vegetables and hobos and beer. Down here on the city's near east side, under the bridges and close to the river, is a gathering of warehouses, wholesale outlets, markets, and other workaday places where you might shoot it out in a dark Raymond Chandler novel: a place brooding, like it might like to be somewhere else.

It's that kind of feeling on that kind of day, and as I sit waiting for Steve Turnsen, chief partner in "Fun Hogs, Inc.," owners of the Produce Row Café, I think about my grandfather's cronies, the Croats, Serbs and Italians who in the old days came down here to meet the trainloads of grapes that would make their dark red wine. Grapes came up from California in the fall; Turnsen came down one fall from Seattle to study English at Lewis & Clark College, later dropped out and with his six partners bought the Produce Row Café from that ubiquitous Portland entrepreneur, Mike McMenamin, in 1978.

Slouching forth from the kitchen where lunch is being prepared, Turnsen slumps into a booth with a look that says, "It was a great idea at the time, but now it's a lot of hard work and…well, I guess it's okay…."

Just tired, maybe.

A thin, dark-bearded man of 41, Turnsen himself will tell you that the café has gone from being the second-most-popular tavern in Portland—"There used to be just us and The Goose"(Bud Clark's Goose Hollow Inn), he says—to a still-popular drinking spot where business is still good but leveled off some, mostly because there is a lot more competition than in the past.

Not that Produce Row has gone stale or flat by any means. It still has one of the largest selections of beer found in any Portland tavern: 27 beers on tap and 150 varieties of bottled beer from around the world, as well as a full repertoire of Portland and other Northwest microbreweries.

While fully half of the four-page menu is devoted to beer (four columns in small type), on other pages are wines, including champagne and hard cider, some interesting soft drinks and, of course, food—mostly sandwiches, hot and cold, salads, salsa, chili and soup of the day.

"When McMenamin had it, back in the early '70s," Turnsen explains, "it was the first place in town with all these imported beers, and that really made our reputation. About that time the small breweries started up and things really took off. People were looking for something different. Then the 'tavern scene' eventually evolved into the 'microbrew-pub scene,' and the older places began hunkering down trying to keep afloat."

Another concern recently is competition between taverns and restaurants for what Turnsen calls "the entire entertainment dollar." "It used to be you could go out, have dinner and a couple of drinks, go to a show, a concert or sporting event, and return later for a few before going home. Now, the cost of one Blazer game can wipe out your budget.

"And," he adds," people don't drink like they used to, especially with the tougher laws against drunk driving—which is a good thing. You have to serve more food, and the food has to be good. You can't get away with just tavern food anymore."

Survival also depends on special attractions, like happy hours on Friday and an outdoor beer garden, as well as live music every Saturday ($2 cover) and Monday night and a Summer Jazz Series on Sunday nights from May to October.

Despite Turnsen's implied ennui—and maybe it's too early, or a bad day—Produce Row Café remains a warm and friendly spot which fulfills its original intent: to be a pleasant and charming incongruity set down amid a tough, pragmatic environment. Once off the street, which rattles and bangs a lot, there are soft lights, warm wood walls and a pub-like atmosphere enhanced by a phalanx of old-fashioned tap handles and those mirrored signs you see in Britain—an oasis in a place of commerce.

Produce Row can accommodate 75 customers at its tables and booths, and Turnsen oversees a staff of 15, who like him have plans to stay. "I have zero interest in starting a new place right now," he confesses, saying he relies now on old customers and a long-standing reputation of keeping things intact. "The reason I'm still going is because I have some pretty loyal followers who keep coming on down here," he says, looking out at the gray morning. "These people pass the word along, a new crowd appears, and…well, we'll be here for a while."

Renner's Grill & Lounge

7819 S.W. Capitol Highway
503-246-9097

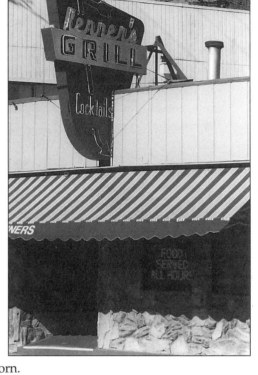

After thirteen years of not visiting the bar where I drank the last serious drink of my life, I walk into Renner's to be greeted by the bartender, who asks simply, "Where you been?"

I sigh because it's like coming home. And because it's like that in Renner's, a confirmed workingman's bar that has been a landmark in Multnomah Village since sometime in the 1920s—but Renner's only since Bessie and Milo Renner put up their sign back in 1939, a year after I was born.

The bartender, Jerry Moe (who has since retired), grins at my order of "Diet Coke," and soon returns with a dark cola glass redolent with the sterner stuff from Tennessee.

"No," I explain kindly, whiffing Daniel's favorite son Jack, "I don't do this anymore."

Jerry is wide-eyed and contrite, and soon returns with the real thing. "I'm sorry," she says, embarrassed because she had forgotten.

But I tell her not to be, that it's an honest mistake — though if I'd taken the drink I might be calling two weeks later from a bar in the Tobago Islands. "Doing a geographic," alcoholics call it.

Sipping my Coke, I ask about the people I used to know in my hazy old drinking days: Doc, Mary Ann and Maria; Frank, the crazy architect who used to come in here; the crazier plumber who used to sit at the bar with his big blonde girlfriend; my dad's old buddy Gaylord.

Most of them gone, Jerry says. Dead or lost to other places, though their candles, I imagine, still burn brightly on both ends.

It is the neighborhood I grew up in. When I was a tyke my mother used to haul me to Multnomah in a coaster wagon. My father came on foot, drinking in the taverns of long ago. Around here I went to school, rode my bike and raised teenage hell. Renner's was always here in Multnomah, snug as a bear's lair, its low-ceilinged, wood-paneled presence assuring me that this is how it would always be. All of life's important ceremonies were celebrated here: birthdays, weddings, divorces; job hirings or firings; birth, sickness and health, even death. In the old days Renner's was people, and the people were happy. Around the bar or in the under-the-sidewalk Suburban Room you could eavesdrop on memories, melodies, truck driver tales and the laments of afternoon housewives.

You still can, but it's not quite like before. Steve Langton, whose family has owned the bar and restaurant since 1978, looks back and says, "So many have passed away. It used to be an older community, but most of the oldtimers are gone."

Only 42, but old in the business, Langton speaks fondly of the Renner's where he began working as a young man. He points through the open door to the Village, now Mother-Goosey with antique and book-stores as well as newer, hipper, politically correct places to "do lunch." The Fat City Café is still there across the street, and down the block the venerable old Ship Tavern remains marooned on its steep side street. But these are surrounded now by restaurants that serve up trendy on a bed of ferns and wash it down with coffee drinks and spring water.

Not Renner's, which Langton describes almost defiantly as a "meat and potatoes kind of place," and whose life-threatening menu includes such no-nonsense staples as endurance-contest pancakes, timber-falling ham and eggs, corned beef and cabbage, sandwiches, and a lot of lethal deep-fried stuff, with fish and seafood (always) on Friday. My kids and I have taken meals here and survived so far, and Langton reminds that Renner's is also a family restaurant, open 6:30 a.m. to 2:30 a.m. every day except Christmas.

"People like the atmosphere," Langton adds. "We get couples and families in here. It's a neighborhood tavern, sure, but neighborhoods change. This is a neighborhood in transition. It used to be we'd lose an oldtimer and pick up two or three, but not anymore. And the kids who come in here now? They want gimmicks, games. They want to be enter-tained," Langton says.

But then he adds brightly, "Neighborhoods revive, they come and go. We'll just have to hang on and wait for things to change."

For the time being, Renner's is somewhere between coming and going, its door always open, still snug as a bear's lair, just waiting for newcomers, and perhaps a few oldtimers like me—an old guy from the old neighborhood who has returned to hear the bartender ask, "Where you been?"

Skyline Tavern

8031 N.W. Skyline Blvd.
503-286-4788

On a day when he is alone and the Skyline Tavern is empty, Manager Andy Craig looks out on a view that would have dazzled Cezanne.

From here, on a high lonely spot in Portland's far West Hills, framed by big firs and heavy with afternoon quiet, you can stare out into vast and swirling El Greco skies above the Tualatin Valley below.

If you had to drink here, I think, considering this great, grand view, it would be comptemplatively, reconsidering all the saloons, gin mills and less appealing places visited before, where the city intrudes and perspective is diminished by how many of us there are. Here, though, in the Skyline Tavern, Andy sighs; I sigh, and the world seems right in the afternoon sun.

Is it always this slow? I ask, not wanting more company.

Andy smiles, ambling over from the spectacular view that has held him here for the past three years—out of the fifty that the tavern has been perched here upon its hill. "Business is good and getting better," Andy proclaims, meaning at night and on weekends when the local denizens mingle with flatlanders up from the valley, so that at any time you might find a congregation of construction workers, farmers, office suits and secretaries, suburbanites or those oldtime Portlanders, like me, who remember something about there being an old tavern up on Skyline.

"And the worse the weather, the busier we are," Craig adds, reminding me that snow often comes earlier and longer to places like this, up high. "People come to play in the snow; they come on skis or four-wheelers, in to get warm or for a stop after Christmas tree cutting."

All natural wood inside beneath overhead fans, the Skyline has its requisite funny signs—"No brains, no service," "All Whining Strictly Prohibited"—as well as darts, pinball, pool and ping-pong, horseshoes outside, even a barbecue pit available for guests who wish to prepare their own food.

There are no lottery games, but the tavern advertises a "Karaoke-Video-Sing-Along-System" for comic relief, as well as a modest paperback library for the occasional bibliophile.

The Skyline is just plain old beer and wine, with 50 bottled beers, including some good Northwest labels, as well as the usual salty snacks.

Is there a kitchen?

"We don't want one," Craig says flatly, the "we" a reference to the tavern's owner, Irene Moberly, who lives in a house next door.

Alive in the heart of Irene's recently renovated, one-bedroom home is the tavern's soul: Irene and her two companions, a restless, wary-eyed Doberman and a parrot named Chico. A short, indomitable woman of 71, Irene has survived three husbands and a career in Portland taverns spanning too many years. She and her late husband bought the Skyline in 1972, remodeled it over the years, and she says she will remain here until the end.

Which may be some time, since Irene is a tough, half-Jewish woman born in Frankfurt, Germany, who with her first husband barely managed to evade Hitler's genocide. Her husband was one of only 33,000 persons to survive a concentration camp.

"I know how to speak German," Irene says without an accent, then cuts her eyes coldly, "but I don't like to."

Her maiden name, interestingly, is Dreyfus, and she explains how she is related to Alfred Dreyfus, the Jewish French Army officer convicted unjustly of treason by an anti-Semitic court martial and sent to Devil's Island in 1895. The cause célèbre inspired French author Emile Zola's impassioned defense, "J'Accuse." Dreyfus was eventually retried and acquitted in 1906.

I say it's a small world, and Irene, a history buff, nods and points out a videotape of "The Dreyfus Affair" plucked from public television.

Abruptly, she announces adamantly, "I don't want anything to do with the state," which I relate to her refusal to install lottery games, but which is later revealed as her opinion on states in general, starting with the Nazis. "But I don't want to get into that now," she says firmly, watching Chico methodically field strip the front page of a newspaper with his lethal-looking beak.

"Here, it's different," she explains. "The Skyline is like taverns used to be in Portland, and I've fought to keep it that way. When you have a tavern you have oldtimers, new neighbors and strangers in your midst." People who have lived in these densely wooded hills, even before the tavern, are still her customers, Irene points out, and she is claiming new patrons from the homes springing up everywhere along Skyline Boulevard. "They're used to having the tavern here. They want to keep it quiet and there's very little trouble."

Like the weather, and the glorious view Irene has from her deck, the Skyline's days are as unpredictable as tavern days can expect to be.

"Sometimes Monday acts like Saturday, or sometimes Sunday get to be like Monday...No one ever knows," Irene says. "It doesn't matter though," she adds resignedly, "people come here for the view.

"And the quiet," Irene says softly. "People say we're the quietest tavern in the State of Oregon."

History by the Glass

Stanich's
Ten-Till-One Tavern

East: 4915 N.E. Fremont St.
503-281-2322
West: 5627 S.W. Kelly St.
503-246-5040

Steve Stanich sinks his choppers into a good-looking hamburger the size of a catcher's mitt, and after chewing for a while wipes his lips and proclaims: "Still tasty after all these years!"

This is after lunch, when most of the civilians have left burping and picking their teeth from Stanich's West down on Southwest Kelly Street, near John's Landing, and Stanich has just had a phone conversation with his father George, patriarch of the family and founder of the Stanich empire back in 1949.

The conversation went something like this: "Listen, Dad, you don't have to tell me everything! I am forty-seven years old, for God's sake!"

But hey! Anyone who knows George and has withstood one of the old Serbian's famous arguments (never argue with a Serbian…or a Croatian, for that matter) will know that Steve is better off listening to the old man.

For it was George, after all, who took a small sleepy tavern on Portland's Northeast Fremont Street, added a grill and, spicing it lavishly with "adversarial conversation," concocted the famous "Stanich Burger" whose slurp is now heard around the world.

In a headline emblazoned among other newspaper clippings that festoon the walls of the Stanich flagship on Fremont Street, read: "Yugoslavian Envoy Makes Portland Tavern Call."

And there in a photograph is George, all chummy with the (former) Yugoslav ambassador, George's good old friend, former Portland Mayor and Oregon Governor Neil Goldschmidt (who once lived down the street), and a gathering of some beefy Balkan-looking guys we aren't too sure about.

What we are told, however, is that newscaster Dan Rather once stopped here on his way to the airport; hoop star Michael Jordan buys a bunch of burgers when he is in town; as well as scores of others, young, old, local and tourist, famous and infamous, who frequent what Steve calls the "ultimate sports bar."

"It's more of a 'Cheers' deal," he explains, his dark brow still brooding after his father's phone call. "More like the sports bars of the '50s and '60s. We've had the same theme since we opened in 1949."

And the same juke box, apparently. Hard enough finding an old fashioned juke box anymore, let alone one like Stanich's, filled with the likes of Frank, Tony, Doris and other permanent residents of Memory Lane.

There are knotty pine walls, good old beer signs, pool tables, silly signs—"Booze and work don't mix, prevent accidents, quit work!" and such—squeezed in among "Rah! Rah!" school pennants that, from their profusion, must represent every college or university in the Western world.

And, significantly, above the bar a drawing of a congenial, plump-cheeked George drawn by an artist who must have caught George on an amiable day.

Back in the dim, antediluvian days of the late '50s, when I first met George in what was then his old "Ten-Till-One Tavern," I became familiar with his style after dropping by after working swing shift.

As he did until recently, George would stand at the end of the bar, smoking interminable Lucky Strikes while holding court and stuffing customers with Stanich Burgers as he led them into unwinnable arguments as entangling as Balkan politics.

"He'd hook 'em, give them five or six beers, then reverse his argument," says Steve, gulping huge concluding bites of his father's massive creation.

"They'd leave, get halfway home and start thinking, then come back to make a last point. Then he'd serve 'em more beer and switch his argument back around again."

Arguments were nourished on the Ten-Till-One "Special," billed immodestly as "The World's Greatest Hamburger," a behemoth, cardiac-inducing assemblage of hamburger, cheese, ham, bacon, egg, tomatoes, lettuce, pickles, onions—and "etc." All of the highest quality, the beef being 100 percent ground chuck, 15–16 percent fat—"for good taste," Steve emphasizes while chewing heartily.

Steve, who began Stanich's West in 1987, says the famous sandwich was inspired by the earlier ham and egg "Fat Man" cheeseburgers once conceived by the Sandy Hut, a restaurant and bar over on Northeast Sandy Boulevard.

"Everybody's copied the burger," he adds, "but few know the right consistency and how they are put together. There is also an art to eating a Stanich Burger," Steve adds with a sober Serbian face that makes you listen closely.

"You pick it up in two hands, and once you start eating you don't put it down."

Nor can you, since its girth makes it almost a physical impossibility, he might have added for the unwary.

But in a culture where fat and red meat have become anathema, doesn't Stanich feel some responsibility to an increasingly health-conscious clientele?

Steve, a former football player and coach who displays a middle-aged man's post-seasonal capacious girth, growls brusquely, "Listen. Serbians don't worry about it."

And again, "Listen," he adds, making his point with a Balkan strong-mindedness that would make his old man proud, "a lot of people wouldn't be as healthy without a Stanich Burger!"

A former teacher and football coach at Tigard High School, Steve now coaches part-time at Lewis & Clark College, has a wife, Debi, three kids and a love for a business dedicated to good food, a friendly atmosphere and, as he states loyally, "keeping my father's name going."

While a few Portland taverns and restaurants have achieved such legendary venerability, Stanich's has maintained its quality and business by remaining entrenched in the city's healthy and constantly recycled close-in neighborhoods.

Out on Fremont Street Stanich's is feeding a second generation raised or moved into the old neighborhood, while in south Portland they are enticing customers from not only the neighborhood, which is experiencing a vibrant gentrification, but also from the surrounding suburbs: commuters, men and women, young and old, and kids during certain hours of the day.

It should be pointed out that during Prohibition many of Portland's Serbs, Croats and Italians were (among others) bootleggers, and despite their often combative stances on issues of the day, their skills at barkeeping seem almost an ethnic inheritance.

At Stanich's, business is about 75 percent food, the rest beer and wine (the rest sports and...perhaps arguments?), and Steve says he has no immediate plans to change.

"I have a good clientele, why change the format?" he insists.

Sylph-like wimps who lack a death wish and prefer alternatives to the formidable Stanich Burger may find their appetites and consciences assuaged by offerings of less formidable burgers, as well as other kinds of sandwiches, salads and such.

But, surprisingly, no pizza, usually the traditional *pièce de résistance* of the proclaimed hard-core sports bar.

Steve explains this with a succinct, no-nonsense comment (what else?) that reveals once more his irrepressible Balkan heritage.

"People ask me sometimes why we don't have pizza," he says in the manner of a man accepting a challenge. "But listen, we don't have onion rings either. We don't have onion rings, but remember, the Ringside (a venerable Portland steak house famous for its onion rings) doesn't have Stanich Burgers."

We will certainly remember—and we will certainly ponder Stanich's arcane reasoning that "a lot of people wouldn't be as healthy without a Stanich Burger."

At least we know now that Serbians don't worry about it.

Twilight Room

5242 N. Lombard St.
503-283-5091

According to random theory, if given typewriters (or word processors these days) a million hardworking chimpanzees might eventually pound out the great works of Shakespeare.

Yet while odds remain slim that a new edition of "Hamlet" might reappear under the byline of someone named "Bongo," those who remember the scribbled-over walls and ceiling of Doug Penner's Twilight Room, a hangout for University of Portland students since the late 1940s, might consider the possibilities.

For buried under layers of paint applied during a recent renovation are the sprawled scrawls of several generations, a trove for cultural anthropologists who someday might be called upon to interpret such arcane graffiti as "Gary Loves Twinkie, 1953," "Mickey Mouse is a Rat!" or the more lyrical, "Show me now who is a swinger of birches..."

And we are surprised when Penner, a pleasant bearded man, expresses no remorse for the disappearance of this remembrance of things past, an archive within whose spontaneous outpourings might be contained an elusive clue to the meaning of life.

"Nah, it was up there long enough," Penner says carelessly, himself a UP graduate who once played guard on the university's last football team, and who has owned the popular North Portland tavern, now with partner Jim McKenna, since 1961.

He explains how the graffiti tradition got started; how on one night a year after graduation UP students were allowed to come in and scribble their names on the walls.

"Eventually things got out of hand, however," Penner says. "I figured they must've been engineering students," he elaborates with a chuckle. "All year all they did was study, then one night they come in and go crazy. But," he sighs, "I guess it was our fault for letting them in."

Nevertheless, the Twilight Room remains a popular hangout for UP students and faculty—"Even the university president comes in from time to time," Penner explains—as well as regular denizens of this solid, working-class neighborhood: industrial workers, small businessmen, residents of course—including recently a healthy influx of young homeowners priced out of Portland's more upscale suburbs.

"For example, we see a lot of homeowners now from southwest Portland," claims Penner, 64, a long-time neighborhood booster who lives five blocks away, "and of the seven North Portland neighborhoods, University Park enjoys the lowest crime rate."

The university is a catalyst for preserving what Penner describes as the community's small-town atmosphere, a feeling that also pervades the clean, ill-lighted ambiance of the Twilight Room.

Basically, the Twilight Room is a no-frills neighborhood tavern that features "burgers and brew," three pool tables, canned music and, inevitably, the lucrative accessibility of lottery games.

"The menu we devised ourselves," Penner explains, referring to his identical twin brother Dean, now living in the East, who helped him start in the business. Featured are burgers, hot dogs and a variety of other sandwiches, salads, snacks, soups and a fiery chili, all of it to be washed down with beer, wine and soft drinks. There are 22 beers on tap, including labels from 17 microbreweries—and, oh yes, there is a kids' menu, since the tavern allows minors in a segregated area until 9 p.m.

"They have to be seated where they can't see the gambling games," Penner says with a grin that acknowledges Oregon's sometimes esoteric liquor laws. "When I was a kid (and when I was too, I remind him), kids could go into taverns and sit right up at the bar," Penner says, though we both know it's much better now than in the past.

Penner looks out onto busy Lombard Street and the traffic passing by. A native of the sleepy Willamette Valley farming community of Mt. Angel, he has been married to his wife Janet, an actress, for 35 years. Just across the street his son Chris, 33, in league with Janet, operates the legendary Portsmouth Club Lounge, along with the adjacent Italian restaurant.

Established so firmly into the community, his son and wife close by, his house down the street near his old alma mater, Penner is a happy man with no immediate plans to retire. If within the walls and ceiling of the Twilight Room are buried the chronicles of the neighborhood's past, a cheerful and optimistic Penner would rather look toward the future.

"Everybody wants to talk about yesterday, how it was in the 'good old days,' " he says. "But not me. I don't want to live in the past."

He could write it on the wall: "Doug loves the Twilight Room, 1961...?"

The Vat & Tonsure

822 S.W. Park Ave.
503-227-1845

Hoping beyond experience that some things will never change, I enter the Vat & Tonsure Tavern to find that all is well; that this cozy, melodic and quite delicious bit of cosmopolitan Portland remains alive and well downtown.

For those of us who used to tryst here, and for those who do so now, "The Vat," as we know it, is a civilized refuge from the pitiless hubbub outside. Its booths are tall, dark and deep, patrons are bathed in classical music upstairs and down, you can smoke anywhere, the food is wonderful—and the 41-page wine list is the longest in town.

I can remember one cold, rainy midweek afternoon some years ago when I was keeping company with a female colleague in a booth upstairs, while all around us, upstairs and down, The Vat's secluded booths were filled with couples murmuring quietly.

Into the indolent atmosphere of long looks, sighs and single, softly unfolding roses burst suddenly a well-dressed middle-aged man who, after finding the center of the floor, whirled with his arms in the air like an impresario and shouted, "My God! Doesn't anyone work anymore?"

"Ah yes!" says The Vat's owner and chef, Rose-Marie Barbeau-Quinn, a twinkle in her eyes for memories of the past, the romance and *gemutlichkeit* created and enhanced by Rose-Marie and her late husband, Mike Quinn.

A plump, rosy-cheeked woman in a long white apron, Rose-Marie makes you think of how your grandmother might have looked when she was young, pretty and just off the boat from the Old Country: blonde hair escaping from a bun, eyes sparkling with good humor yet holding a loving sadness in memory of Mike, who was only 52 when he died of a heart attack in 1994.

From the booth where we are sitting Rose-Marie looks over at the bar. Behind it is an enlarged photograph of Mike in profile, bearded and thoughtful, looking out into a gray Portland day.

Many of us remember him from Portland State College, back in the 1960s when we were English majors together. Then, he burned with an intellectual intensity that masked a playful sense of humor, which, with his love of music, would someday overwhelm Rose-Marie's heart.

Taking her eyes away, she says with a singular poignancy, "I will never meet anyone like him again."

Because this is a love story that opens during an opera, it is appropriate to begin in Vienna, during a performance of Wagner's "Parsifal" in 1967.

"Mike told me later, 'Christ! How could we not meet? That damned opera was six hours long!' "

Rose-Marie, a Reubenesque French-Canadian woman, was in Vienna to study singing under a Canadian government grant, while Mike was immersing himself in the cultural attributes of the Austrian capital.

It was in Vienna also that Rose-Marie, a soprano who still sings in concerts around Portland, began learning to cook.

"We both liked to cook, we liked good wine, and after we found an apartment we would often cook for friends who kidded us about opening a restaurant someday," Rose-Marie says, making the story short.

"When we returned we opened here and it has remained the same ever since."

Mike opened in the mid-1970s, moving into a space formerly occupied by a popular gaslighted downtown bar known as "The Gay (in the traditional sense) '90s," where Mike had worked while in college.

Before that, Rose-Marie will tell you, there was a restaurant here known as "Adele's," which featured German-Jewish cuisine and was once one of the most popular restaurants in town.

As is the Vat & Tonsure today, though The Vat maintains a tavern license so that beer and wine, including labels from a number of local microbreweries and wineries, may be sold to go.

"We were the first tavern to sell Bridgeport Ale," Rose-Marie points out, "and we have several other local beers along with a number of imported labels, but...we have 850 different wines!" she says proudly, thumping down a catalogue-hefty wine list.

Most of these wines are from France, Italy, Spain and Portugal, "But we also have a lot of Oregon wines," Rose-Marie says, "but none from California. Mike didn't like California wines because he was dead set against using wines labeled with place names...and for other reasons, one of which was he was also against those who claimed they were 'making wine.' He considered wine an art form."

For two months each summer, Mike and Rose-Marie would close The

Vat and tour Europe, allowing themselves to improve on their already impressive knowledge of wine and to make friends with owners of some of the world's most renowned vineyards.

Mike's love of wine is represented in the tavern's name, which Rose-Marie admits is puzzling to many customers.

"We wanted to have no name, but the Oregon Liquor Control Commission wouldn't allow that, and we had to come up with something fairly quickly. Mike remembered a drawing by the 19th century German cartoonist Wilhelm Busch, a little monk (a monk's halo-like haircut is called a "tonsure") praying over a vat of wine, and we used that as our logo. We were going to change it eventually, but the name just stuck."

The Vat currently has seven waiters, all young men and all knowledgeable about wine (and music, which they often choose for The Vat's background), and to those who sometimes criticize her for not having women employees, Rose-Marie rolls her eyes and says, "Yes, we do have a woman working here. Me! One woman is enough."

Small, intimate, yet refreshingly unpretentious, The Vat is a favorite luncheon spot for downtown denizens, business and professional people, while at night, Rose-Marie says, "You might get anybody."

A lot of people come in for dinner before shows or concerts, and later for a glass of beer or wine, maybe some bread and cheese, afterwards.

"We're open from 11:30 a.m. to 2:30 a.m.—or as along as someone's here," she says cheerfully. "In the late afternoon and evenings we get a lot of people who just come in and hang out, drinking and listening to the music."

It used to be that Mike had a sign that read, "This entire establishment is a smoking area." Smoking is still allowed, though Marie said Mike had quit about a year before his heart attack.

The Vat's menu is simple yet elegant, subject to Rose-Marie's whims: usually Cornish game hens, salads, lamb and pork chops, Irish stew; sometimes a pork roast, as well as seasonal dishes, including prawns, halibut, trout and other items.

There is also espresso coffee, a brew with much authority, as well as soft drinks and non-alcholic beer.

Taking a break from lunch, Rose-Marie looks over at Mike's picture again and reminisces, while haunting music from Kevin Burke's Irish violin swells into the room.

The Vat has its own grand piano, and often visiting musicians, many who knew Mike and Rose-Marie from before, come in to eat and drink, often to sing and play.

Then she looks back and says how, after being together for 25 years, after planning to get married in 1992, they were finally married at Mike's bedside just before he died.

Almost on cue, the music fades and Rose-Marie breaks a great warm smile.

"Life has been different without Mike but I've learned to live with it. It was murder at first, running the restaurant and learning all the wines, but I knew I had to find a way through, and often I just faked it, though I feel that Mike is here in the restaurant with me every day.

"And I'm still here," she says confidently, "missing him every day. I'll never find anyone like Mike again."

The Veritable Quandary

1220 S.W. 1st Ave.
503-227-7342

No wider than its window and front door, the fourteen-by-ninety-nine-foot Veritable Quandary is an old-brick vestige of gaslight days, when horse-drawn carriages clopped up and down Southwest First Avenue.

Dennis King, who opened the bar in 1970, claims the building's heritage reaches back to the 1880s, and points proudly to a twenty-two-foot bar that traveled here on a sailing ship around the Horn and once graced the old Gay '90s tavern on Park Avenue.

Somewhere around here, he says, there's an old photograph showing that Jake's Original Crawfish Restaurant was once directly across the street, adjacent to an old fire station whose engines were pulled by horse teams, and down the street…King, a native Portlander, goes on like that for a while.

How the Veritable Quandary got its name has nothing to do with how King manages to operate a full restaurant and bar in a space that, when crowded, would make it difficult to swing even a small cat. "I must have gone through dozens of names when I first bought the place," he said. "Then one night I was drinking up at the old Gay '90s when I overheard someone mumble in their beer, 'I'm in a veritable quandary.'"

"I was in a kind of funky mood that night, and it just seemed to fit," he says, adding thoughtfully, "I think it comes from *Alice in Wonderland* or something."

(When reading through a first draft of this essay he also reminded me that it was not "Quandry," as I had misspelled it throughout, admonishing, "God, Paul! You're a journalist and should know better," though adding warmly, "but, hell, it gets spelled wrong 75 percent of the time."

Beneath its high ceilings, fitted between the Quandary's warm, narrow, natural brick walls baked from one of Portland's now-extinct brickyards, are a full bar, booths, tables, and a tiny gazebo-like kitchen added several years ago, when King expanded into an outdoor garden terrace, an oasis against the traffic swirling by.

The atmosphere is Old Portland, but King describes the menu as "New York Café," offering pasta dishes and (King's eyes brighten carnivorously), "Lots of meat: beef, chicken and fish…we also bake our own desserts," he adds in the manner of a once brash barkeep gentled to restaurateur.

Along with the food, acknowledging that his customers are inclined to drink more moderately and raise less hell than in the old days, King has varied the musical offerings to suit the tastes of his customers. "In the old days," he says, "I used to control the speed of the crowd by being my own disc jockey." His strategy was a kind of melodious psychological warfare, and King breaks a rare and cunning grin to explain, "I'd stack the juke box with meticulous care. I might start the night with, say, some Rolling Stones, then conclude with 'The War of 1812 Overture.' You know, just to calm things down."

Now, however, having acquiesced to the exigencies of "trendy," there is live music a couple of nights a week ("nothing hard, mind you," King says) to please a crowd whose taste has changed considerably in recent years.

While the Quandary still sees many of the same reliable downtown types as in years before—lawyers, judges and other "legals," and politicians from the government offices up the street—there has been an infusion of young, bright-eyed initiates on their maiden voyages to career fullfillment.

Denizens, those who arrived at the outset and whose dreams remain fixed on some distant, unattainable star, are still in evidence as reminders of what drinking in Portland used to be about. When I still counting coup in many of the city's bars, the Quandary often held me in its embrace. Usually arriving at about the time King's musical offerings were rolling over to Beethoven, I would sit, sip and let the music pour over me, soothing the battles in my head and heart.

It was that kind of place.

During my years of sobriety, I would run into King occasionally on the street and always be greeted warmly. "Listen," he would say, "just because you gave up drinking doesn't mean you can't come in anymore." Today, King, a ruddy-faced, red-haired man of 52, need not remind me that we are both older in an age of young drinkers and things aren't like they used to be; good for me but somewhat dismaying to a man who has always been a gracious host with a reputation for running a bar that was not only a conversation piece, but a place for good conversation.

It is something we both miss.

Nevertheless, for romantics who appreciate the Quandary's Old Portland ambiance, it remains a place to sit and consider on a quiet afternoon. At a river-view table, I follow King's eyes across the terrace with its fiercely blooming wisteria, both of us enjoying the sturdy presence of the Hawthorne Bridge, a venerable 86-year-old structure that somehow symbolizes Portland. King looks at me and comments emotionally, "I love that old bridge. I've looked at it for 30 years and never tire of the view."

And somehow, for two friends, native Portlanders reflecting on the sweet light of our middle years, that seems to say it all.

History by the Glass

Wanker's Corner Saloon & Café

2509 Borland Rd.
Tualatin, OR 97062
503-638-4891

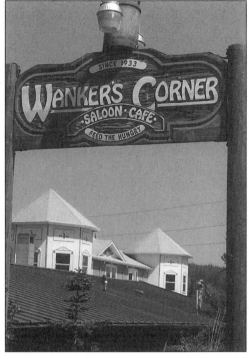

When the employees at Wanker's Corner Saloon & Café urge you playfully to "grab your nuts" (if you feel like it), they are of course referring to the bowls of free roasted peanuts whose shells cover the floor in a crunchy tide.

Not surprisingly, Wanker's Corner doles out some 25,000 pounds of peanuts each year, allowing the little newspaper it prints as part of its menu to proclaim Wanker's as the "Goober Pea Capital of the West" (goobers, of course, being peanuts in a Southern interpretation).

The little paper, about the size of the bottom of a birdcage, also lets you know that there has been a tavern on this corner since 1933 (the year Prohibition ended), when beer began being served in the back of a grocery store across the street.

Oregon Geographic Names lists the tavern's location as Wanker's (prounounced WANG-KERS) Corner, Oregon, named for an early settler.

However, J. L. Maixner, the tavern's owner, prefers an Australian term, "wanker," a ribaldry best interpreted outside of mixed company, and when (if you feel like it) you are eating peanuts.

Not that Maixner is Australian. No way. Maixner is a native Oregonian born and raised on top of Cooper Mountain, just west of Beaverton and overlooking the Tualatin Valley; a graduate of Beaverton High School and well known for years as the proprietor of some of the most popular (and now defunct) taverns in Portland: after learning the business at The Faucet, legendary for its turtle races, Maixner went on to own the Wurst Haus, a favorite of college students back in the '60s; the Stein Haus out in "deep southeast" Portland; and a place called Scooter McQuade's, as well as Banana's Café and Bar.

This from a guy who was an Eagle Scout and wanted to be a cop.

"I've always felt like a cop," Maixner says. "I got into the tavern business accidentally. I was 21 and studying police science when I began work at The Faucet. I never went back."

Moving back and forth as he talks, Maixner hems and haws. He is a man with a Hawaiian tan below a shock of receding blonde hair and looks maybe ten years younger than his 54 years.

He also doesn't look like a guy from around here.

Tell him that, and Maixner grins and leans over a belly kept trim on his Nordic-Track.

"People come in and say to me, 'Hey! You're from California, right?'

"I say, 'No, I'm from right around here.'

"They say, 'Come on! You're kidding, right?'

"I say, 'No, I swear…I grew up just over the hill.'

"But they persist. 'Come on, man! Where you from?'

"Finally I give in and say, 'Okay. I'm from Hermosa Beach.'

"And they get all excited and say, 'Hey! I knew it!'

"Californians! They gotta believe everybody's from someplace else."

On a raw day when there is rain and hail and thunder outside, Wanker's Corner is a cozy oasis, a simple bunker-like building fitted out in the fashion of a large cabin set somewhere far away. The heavy furniture appears to have been chainsawed directly from a tree, while most of the space on the natural walls and ceiling is covered with signs of all ilk; odd, rusting pieces of farm equipment; advertisements for beer; all of it put together with a distinct Australian accent ("Strine," if you're a purist).

Outside the entrance a small plaque advises, "Street girls bringing sailors into the hotel must pay for room in advance," while inside there are signs warning of kangaroo and wombat crossings, with one reading: "Wanker's Corner Saloon employees are highly trained professionals— do not try this at home!"

Maixner's love of things Australian was acquired during several trips down under, where he fell in love with the country and its free-wheeling, irreverent, beer-drinking population, which reminds him of the States back in the 1950s.

In tribute, Wanker's puts out its own microbrew, "Outback Ale"— "Tawny in colour, fresh roasted aroma, with a delicate flavour and a smooth finish"—as well as a line of shirts, hats, panties, lighters, coffee mugs, beer glasses and what-have-you, offered blatantly around the confession (on the menu right under, "Things smell different to a midget in an elevator"): "You don't think we 'make it' selling food, do you? Hell no! Our main biz is selling EXTRA CRAP!—Authentic Wankerwear Equipment."

Like most taverns these days, Wanker's Corner has become a food place with a menu that, if not extensive, is eclectic, with sandwiches found under the distinctive "Moo," "Oink" and "Peep" categories; there is a "Splash" tuna offering, as well as an impressive array of pizzas, salads and some select Mexican specialties; sometimes a combo of all of the above, like the "Chicken Pizza Ranchero."

What you really have to see is the "Nacho Supreme" (served after 2 p.m. weekdays and all day on weekends), a monster bowlful of chips, refried beans, cheese, olives, jalapeños, salsa, green onions, sour cream and guacamole, which, on the day we were there, was virtually attacked and devoured by no fewer than six people.

Maixner chuckles, "Yeah, they're big."

And so is the beer selection, which along with Outback Ale includes local and domestic brews, Australian and other foreign labels.

Essentially, Wanker's Corner is a beer tavern gone a bit "round the bend," reflecting the humor, imagination and spontaneity of Maixner, who has owned the place since 1985.

It is Maixner too who writes, edits and publishes the menu-newspaper, and who provides the saloon's "Wanker Wit," aphorisms of universal wisdom such as, "All other things being equal, fat people use more soap," "Not one shred of evidence supports the notion that life is serious," and my favorite, "When you dance with a bear, you can't sit down when you're tired."

Maixner, on the other hand, seems to be a man who could dance a bear into the ground.

Along with his tavern business, he is the owner of "J. L. Maixner's Movie Art of Portland," through which he buys, sells and trades cowboy memorabilia from an era he calls the "silver screen cowboys": Roy Rogers, Gene Autry, Hopalong Cassidy and others, many of them names no one but Maixner seems to have heard of.

Maixner claims Roy is a longtime friend, and each November 5th the tavern has a "Roy Rogers Birthday Party" to celebrate Roy's birth (as Leonard Slye) in Ohio.

"I got started when I was a boy selling seeds door to door," Maixner explains. "My first prize was a pair of Roy Rogers binoculars, which I still have, and I just couldn't stop. Now I have one of the largest collections of Roy Rogers memorabilia in the country."

He adds somewhat wistfully, "I tried to get Roy up here more than once, but he's getting pretty old now and doesn't like to travel."

Lured by Wanker's Corner tee-shirts, sold around the world, Maixner gets visitors from all over, even Australians, and including a contingent of sports and other celebrities who play in the annual Fred Meyer Challenge at the nearby Oregon Golf Club.

"Personally, I don't consider this a sports bar," Maixner says. "I never got into sports, and I'm not a sports fan, but there are times during the year, the World Series or Superbowl, when we can't help it."

In good weather months the tavern opens up into an outdoor beer garden, where on a clear day there are bucolic views of farms, fields, rolling hills and trees, but also an awareness of the suburban sprawl leaking over from Lake Oswego to the north.

Maixner says he doesn't mind, since most of his customers come from Portland and the suburbs, especially on weekend nights where there is live music and a line outside the door, but also a cover charge of $1.49. (Wanker's is open from 10 a.m. to midnight during the winter, and in summer to 1 or 2:30 a.m., depending on the whim of the owner.)

Those put off by the modest weekend cover charge, however, are reminded that all cover charge proceeds are donated to the Oregon Food Bank, which has received over $50,000 from the tavern since 1990.

"What began as a joke during the spring of 1990," Maixner writers in his paper, "now has the food bank laughing all the way to the bank."

Maixner's Eagle Scout beneficence is also evident in a concern for his staff of 20 devoted employees, his nice-tough guy solicitude reflected in signs that encourage tipping, with the admonishment: "Don't stiff your servers. They don't get mad, they get even."

And for his customers, who come for the beer, food and to "grab their nuts" and throw the shells on the floor, Maixner provides this quote from Henry Lawson, the Australian Walt Whitman: "Beer makes you feel the way you oughta feel without beer!"

For himself, Maixner is quite content. Business is good, he has a new apartment in Hawaii, Roy calls now and then, and his ambitions, so far, have been fulfilled.

Maixner smiles. "People have asked me why I stay in the business. I tell them, 'When I get up in the morning, I want to go to work.' "

Happy trails to you!

The White Eagle Café & Saloon

836 N. Russell St.
503-282-6810

Then there was the day not too long ago when the clock just flew off the wall.

"It's that damned ghost," says Chuck Hughes. "That's the fourth time he's done that. I came in one morning and he'd taken all the bottles off the bar and put them on the floor."

Or is it a "she?" A prostitute named Rose, killed long ago by a jealous lover when the White Eagle Café & Saloon had a bordello upstairs and the 90-year-old establishment was part of the once independent City of Albina?

"All I know is there's a ghost in here," says Hughes, a small wiry man of 53 who has owned the North Portland tavern since 1978.

"And there could be as many as two or three," he adds matter-of-factly. "I know for sure there's one upstairs, and I had a parapsychologist come in for lunch one time and tell me there was something 'evil' in the basement. She didn't have to tell me, I found that out myself."

Hughes tells of being rocked in his cot when sleeping over in his office downstairs ("I don't do that anymore," he says firmly); of spectral hands placed on his shoulders; visions on the stairs ("like dust whirling"); of foul smells, sudden drops in temperature, and the sounds of a woman sobbing, heard by a number of customers.

We hunker down and Hughes goes on. This is fascinating stuff. Especially when, even on a bright and sunny day, the inside of the White Eagle has all the charms of a crypt.

True, it's cozier at night, when a band is playing and customers are gathered beneath warm lights, but a trip back to the Eagle's lonely John can have you looking over your shoulder and listening for sounds you don't want to hear.

A long, high-ceilinged brick box built as a saloon in 1905, the White Eagle has (except for one year, 1936, when it was the Blue Eagle) retained the name ever since.

According to a history Hughes has carefully tracked and compiled, the original owners were two immigrants, Barney Sobolaski and William Hryasho, and from the looks of things there have been few changes since.

Except for the gloomy upstairs, where the empty whorehouse has become a house of spirits, and the downstairs, where Hughes shares his office with an unnamed evil, the saloon remains basically the same.

The original backbar, a massive and mirrored dark-wood classic shipped to Portland from the East, stretches some 30 feet along one wall; the floor is original tile mosaic blending into hardwood, atop which is a scattering of tables and chairs.

Hughes keeps a clutch of lottery games—"The bands aren't doing it for me anymore," he confesses—hidden discreetly inside a cubicle, next to which is a kitchen providing a menu appropriate for a haunted saloon: sandwiches, salads and burgers, along with "House Delights"—"Tits and Chips" (chicken breasts and fries); fish and chips and stuffed shrimp, and a list of "Nightly Specials."

Since the White Eagle has a full hard liquor and beer bar, drink specials are offered Monday through Thursday.

The White Eagle is closed on Sunday, and Hughes likes to close up on weeknights about 10 p.m. (the ghosts come out around 8 p.m., he says.) On Friday and Saturday nights he stays open until 2:30 a.m., however, and he gets a good crowd in for live music from a variety of bands.

"I used to have a band that played so loud people used to listen to them from their cars out on the street," Hughes says with a rare grin. "They were good, and I had them for years, but they were driving my customers away. Now I have softer stuff: some rock-and-roll, rhythm and blues…It's a lot quieter."

Hughes, who is wearing a White Eagle tee-shirt, is a lot quieter too. A native of Portland, he confessed to being a juvenile delinquent while a student at Benson High, though the Army straightened him out, he says, and after returning from Vietnam he worked for some years at Hyster Corp. before buying the White Eagle.

"I always wanted my own business, and I tried everything, so why not the saloon business?" Hughes explains. "And it wasn't so much that I liked the business, which I originally bought to sell, as I liked the building."

From the outside, the White Eagle's facade expresses a kind of modest magnificence. And even before I knew about the ghosts, the saloon had always conveyed a rather foreboding aspect that makes you wonder if it might not be best to have a drink *before* going inside?

And it could be, too, that there are some leftover vibes from when the White Eagle was a hardcore biker hangout, since its previous owners represented the motorcycle clubs, "The Outsiders" and "Brother Speed."

"At first I had a hell of a time with them," Hughes admits. "then I finally ran them all out. They were too much trouble. Once in a while now, however, I get an old biker who is real polite. Get them one-on-one and they're not so bad."

Today Hughes has what he calls a "nice crowd," working men and women, people from the nearby Union Pacific Railroad yards; there are a lot of artists in the area, as well as city employees and those from the Portland School District offices nearby.

On nights and weekends there's a younger crowd, and occasionally people from anywhere, including foreign lands, lured by the White Eagle's reputation or maybe curious about the bumper stickers and tee-shirts that read, "Where the hell is the White Eagle?"

Others have heard about the ghosts, of course, which Hughes has been battling since the summer of 1981; in August, when he came to work and first found the bottles on the floor. The clock has flown off the wall at least four times since (at this writing).

"One day I went upstairs when it was 100 degrees, and the temperature up there suddenly dropped so it was like an icebox," Hughes says dramatically. "Then I smelled a foul smell, felt hands on my shoulders and my hair stood on end. I can't tell you what it was, but I don't stay here nights anymore."

The lunching parapsychologist, who, Hughes swears, never left the bar downstairs and had never seen the upstairs (it was her first visit), asked for paper and drew a diagram of the White Eagle's second floor.

"She drew everything just as it is," Hughes says convincingly. "She showed me dark spots where things weren't normal up there, then looked me in the eye and said, 'And there's an evil down here.' These ghosts, she said, were trapped between life and death."

Though usually the ghosts don't bother the customers, Hughes says, "I had one customer who totally freaked out." He shrugs, "She said she'd never come back, and I can't say I blame her."

Business is good, however, or at least steady, though Hughes says he has noticed changes in Portland's tavern scene.

"The crowds are easier now, different as night and day. People don't drink as much, and we serve more food. It used to be if I cut someone off they would want to fight. Now they just nod and say I'm doing them a favor. People don't want to get caught drinking and driving."

Like many long-time saloon keepers, Hughes is fond of the White Eagle's customers, who are served by a loyal staff of six employees.

Does he anticipate any changes?

Hughes laughs and looks around.

"Yeah," he says, "I might dust the bar."

More seriously, Hughes proclaims, "I'm totally satisfied here, and I love the building the way it is, ghosts and all. I'm either tired or retired, I don't know what.

"But," he adds, one eye on the clock and leaning closely, "I will tell you one thing. In this place you're always looking over your shoulder."

The Brothers McMenamin

Say "McMenamin" three times real fast, and by the time you get your tongue straightened out the McMenamin Brothers, Mike and Brian, will have probably opened a new pub or brewery somewhere in the Northwest. Since 1973, when Mike McMenamin began in the business, the busy brothers have yet to put a head on a foamy empire of rapidly expanding "brewpubs," taverns, restaurants and theatre-pubs that have encouraged Portland's national reputation as "Beer City."

Created from the McMenamins' daring and imaginative marketing skills, this is now a regional empire whose successful innovations are considered by many as a harbinger of things to come.

So far numbering 34 (fall of 1995), the majority of McMenamins' establishments are concentrated in or near Portland, though recently they have expanded into other parts of Oregon and Washington as well.

A major catalyst was the 1985 opening of the Hillsdale Brewery & Public House in Southwest Portland, the first authentic brewpub to appear in Oregon since Prohibition—a "brewpub" being defined as a combination brewery and pub producing relatively small quantities of distinctive "homemade" ales. Conceived in the McMenamins' own "Captain Neon's Fermentation Chamber" ("famous throughout the cosmos!"), these include five exotic ales praised by aficionados: Terminator Stout, Ruby (raspberry ale), Crystal, Hammerhead and Cascade Head; all of which are made from Northwest grains and hops and exemplify the McMenamins' dedication to the region.

As Mike, a native Portlander, explains, "We wanted to brew a native product, not a British ale, nor a German ale, thus our experimental ways. The only rule in our brewery is that there are no rules."

Nor, it seems, are there any rules against expanding beyond what the McMenamins call "the friendly neighborhoods of Portland."

McMenamin outposts have been firmly established in a number of Oregon cities outside of Portland, as well as in Seattle, where three pubs (with more planned) have been opened, while another overlooks the Columbia River in Vancouver, U.S.A.

The McMenamins' Oregon empire has reached into Portland's suburban communities (Tigard, Beaverton, Sherwood, Hillsboro, Gresham, Clackamas, Oregon City, West Linn and Hillsboro), while in the Willamette Valley a pub is found in Salem (the state capital), with others in the thirsty university towns of Corvallis (Oregon State University) and

Eugene (University of Oregon).

It is east of Portland, however, in the small city of Troutdale—"Gateway to the Columbia River Gorge," Oregon's most popular tourist attraction—that the McMenamins have created their showplace: McMenamins' Edgefield, a unique and exciting resort complex sprawling over 25 acres of what was once the Multnomah County Poor Farm.

Centerpiece of what could be called the McMenamins' "Magic Kingdom" at Edgefield is its Main Lodge. Built in 1911, the renovated structure was once a retirement home of grim Dickensian ambiance, and is now listed on the National Register of Historic Places.

The Main Lodge offers a variety of hotel accommodations, including suites, bed-and-breakfast rooms and an inexpensive hostel, and private rooms are notably free of television sets and telephones—though some might be shared with ghosts who, in one wing at least, according to the McMenamins, occasionally go bump in the night.

Lodge guests and the public may dine in The Black Rabbit Restaurant, which features Northwest cuisine, cocktails, an extensive list of foreign and domestic wines (including Northwest labels), and which is open for breakfast, lunch and dinner seven days a week.

Around the lodge, settled whimsically into former poor farm buildings, are The Power Station Pub and its adjacent Power Station Theater (full-length feature films nightly), and two outdoor pubs: The Little Red Shed (self-proclaimed "smallest pub in North America"), open in summer from Thursday through Sunday, and The Loading Dock Beer Garden & Grill, open everyday during the summer season.

In their 20-barrel Edgefield Brewery, established in 1991 as a regional brewery, the McMenamins produce a variety of handcrafted ales, including Transformer, Ruby, Hammerhead, India Pale Ale and Black Rabbit Porter.

Like all McMenamin brews, these are natural (uncarbonated, unpasteurized) ales, and since they are not bottled or allowed to travel, they are available only on draught in McMenamins' establishments.

The Edgefield Winery is supported in part by the McMenamins' small vineyard, and since 1990 has been bottling a selection of wines whose labels now include Cabernet Sauvignon, Merlot, White Riesling, Chardonnay, Pinot Gris and an award-winning Pinot Noir. The winery also has a tasting room open to the public.

Visitors who linger at McMenamins Edgefield may stroll the extensive grounds, which feature an impressively planted observation garden, vineyards, an outdoor amphitheater and the Corcoran Glassworks, where the fine art of glass blowing may be observed.

In addition, graphic designs and paintings representing the work of some 14 artists are evident throughout the resort, which also hosts a variety of special events: parties, conferences, weddings, banquets, reunions and other activities.

Up close and in person, the brothers McMenamin are a couple of large, friendly, unpretentious guys whose soft-nosed personalities seem incongruous to the hard-nosed business of empire building. That's because both are sustained by a love for their hometown, a firm dedication to what they do and a good-natured confidence in the future.

Mike, the eldest, is a bearded, 44-year-old man who got into the business with the Produce Row Café in 1973, transforming a workaday diner into an atmospheric pub that set a standard for many of Portland's newer drinking establishments. (Since sold, the Produce Row Café still offers one of Portland's largest selections of imported and tailor-made Northwest beers, and its current owners graciously attribute its continued success to McMenamin's foresight.)

A graduate of Jesuit High School, as is his brother Brian, a hefty, clean-shaven man of 33, Mike studied English and political science at Oregon State University in Corvallis, where he began working in small taverns to earn money for school.

"I liked it," he says succinctly. "I enjoyed the atmosphere and the customers and just decided to stay. It has a way of holding on to you."

Eventually, Brian, who had intended to go to law school (their father, Robert McMenamin, is an attorney), came aboard, attracted like his brother to a business he finds challenging as well as fun.

The brothers are sitting at a table in the vast, afternoon-empty Mission Street Theatre & Pub, a massive, elaborately revived brick landmark in Northwest Portland that for decades had been a longshoremen's hiring hall.

Along with serving food and drink beneath a screen flickering with full-length feature films, the building contains the McMenamins' offices, and its carefully renovated interior reflects their dedication to historic preservation. In addition to the Mission and the theater-pub at Edgefield, the McMenamins include the Bagdad Theater & Pub, having transformed the venerable neighborhood movie house so it is now a focal point of the revitalized Hawthorne District in Southeast Portland.

Mike explains, "We've always liked historic spaces. We feel they're important and their preservation is vital to a city's traditions."

Brian interjects, "We also tend to be spontaneous and like to keep experimenting to see what we can do. These old projects are really fun," he adds with a disarming exuberance.

Recently, the McMenamins decided to experiment with Portland's historic Crystal Ballroom, a formerly grand and glorious downtown dance hall whose unique, ballbearing-supported floor has undulated with the beat of dancing feet since 1914. Into this hallowed space, whose refurbished dance floor retains its distinctive bounce, the McMenamins are incorporating a brewpub featuring Crystal Ale, a brew whose name and deep amber color venerate the historic ballroom. The ballroom is expected to be open by fall, 1996.

Another recent project that typifies a commitment to the city's urban neighborhoods is the Kennedy Theater-Pub, which is being installed within the graceful old Kennedy Elementary School building in Northeast Portland, and which should be completed by the summer of 1997. Mike explains how the pub will retain the integrity of the school's elegant white terra cotta facade, while inside transforming a central atrium into an outdoor beer garden.

"Portland," he says, "is a friendly, liveable place that retains its small-town atmosphere. More important, unlike a lot of other cities, its close-in neighborhoods are holding together.

Having been to Europe, the McMenamins acknowledge the small pubs, inns and gasthauses, many serving their own beer, that are part of a centuries-old cultural tradition. "We respect that tradition," Mike says, "but here we have a different culture; we're not even close to the English and German pub atmosphere, nor do we feel we should be."

The McMenamins' pubs rely on good food and good beer; there are no pool tables or lottery games, and Brian emphasizes they are more concerned with providing a "family alternative" to other drinking places. Minors are allowed in McMenamin pubs during mealtime, and some pubs are smoke-free.

"There's more food being served now, and people tend to drink less," Brian says, "but who knows about the future? These things tend to be cyclical, and often there is an unpredictable backlash. Food is big right now, and pool, but that could change back to something else. Who knows? We try to be flexible."

But what about saturation? Do the McMenamins foresee a day when the regional market is simply unable to absorb the currently rapid proliferation of microbreweries?

"I don't think so, "Mike says confidently. "I think you could have a thousand microbreweries in the region, and, because of the small amounts they produce, still have a healthy market."

He adds, "You have to remember that we don't compete with other microbreweries since we distribute only in our own pubs."

"And more than that," Brian interjects, "we make good beer."